CHRONICLES
OF a BOOB

Vol. I

D1176634

Humorous tales of breast cancer, anxiety & gross exaggeration

KAREN McCOOL

Copyright

Copyright Postscript

Wherein I translate confusing copyright lingo into layman's terms.

S O THE COPYRIGHT AREA of the book is where the author or publisher says shit like, "No part of this publication may be reproduced, distributed, or transmitted in any form or by any means, including crayon, tracing paper, or texting it to your friend," but let's face it, it's highly unlikely that I'd catch you doing any of those things, and even if I did, who wants to pay for a fucking copyright attorney? Not I. Then I'd have to go to court, and I bet judges hate when people show up in court wearing jeans and wrinkly "Don't Judge Me" tee shirts. Since that's all I have that's clean right now, and I don't feel like doing laundry, I'll keep it simple and ask that you:

DON'T BE A DICK.

If you'd like to use a short quote from this book for something like … oh … I don't know … let's say a really super awesome Amazon review, first, *thank you!* And second, feel free to quote away, and please send a link to your review to the following email:

karen@chroniclesofaboob.com

Dedication

This book is dedicated to my husband, Fran, who doesn't always laugh at my jokes (though he should, because *I* think they're funny, and we both know who's always right), and who thought this book was a silly idea that would never get published. (But he'd never heard of a little thing called self-publishing. Say *whaaat?!* Ha! In your face!)

I love you, Fran ... and your little dogs, too.

Table of Contents

How to use the "old person assistance section"

THE EVENTS DESCRIBED IN this book actually happened (mostly), and there are, unequivocally, *zero* exaggerations (aside from a smattering of embellishments). Yes, it's all true, except for the parts I made up.

Since roughly half of my readers will likely be folks over the age of seventy (Hi, Mom and Dad!), and I sometimes use terminology that they, as old people, may be unfamiliar with, I've decided to include a helpful hints section at the back of the book, otherwise known as a glossary—or, in this case, the Old Person Assistance Section, referenced within the text as "old ass," for brevity. It's specifically designed for elderly readers who don't understand some of my young and hip lingo. (No, not the kind of hip you're always breaking. I mean hip as in "cool" or "groovy" or "swell.") When you see the phrase "see old ass" anywhere in the text, it means you'll find an explanation of the word or phrase that appears in bold before it, at the back of the book. Look for this drawing:

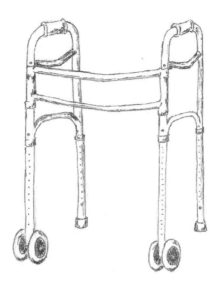

If you're reading this in an ebook format, you can click on each "old ass" term and be taken directly to its glossary definition. Through the clever use of hyperlinks, you can then return to the point in the text where you left off, by clicking on the corresponding glossary term. Let's try it now. Click on this phrase: **glossary example**.

I hope you've figured out how to return here; otherwise, you're still stuck in the glossary. My apologies if you're stuck in the glossary. You might consider waiting for the paperback edition. Until then, please enjoy reading the rest of the glossary.

I suppose only those people who have successfully returned from the glossary are reading this right now, so let's all take a moment to feel superior to those idiots trapped at the end of the book. No outright bullying, just a skosh of silent judging. Now take a moment to reflect on some dumb thing you've done in the past, like that time you blamed your loud fart on a barking tree frog, then realized you were in a fancy restaurant in the middle of Philadelphia.

(And who hasn't, amirite?) Have you remembered your embarrassing moment? Great, now we all feel like idiots.

For those who previously got stuck in the glossary and are now reading the paperback version of this book, the hyperlink effect can be achieved by keeping one finger on this page whilst flipping to the back of the book. Try that now. Also, give yourself a minute to judge all those fuckers who were judging you earlier for getting stuck in the glossary. Those assholes have issues.

Now that I see you're all back, let's move on to the first chapter, sans all judgment, shall we?

Chapter 1

Where to place the hospital bed and other preparations for my death

POSSIBLY THE BEST PART about knowing you're going to die in a few weeks is that you have time to destroy all your old underwear—the panties with the pathetically crispy elastic that's lost all ability to snap back, and the bras that have stretched so far out of shape they're more like windsocks than boob supporters. You also, thankfully, have time to delete any embarrassing entries in your internet browsing history.[1] And if you're really lucky, both of your parents will still be alive, giving you the chance to say all those things that should never be left unsaid—things you want them to know and would regret never having told them, like, "Thanks so much for *not* buying me a bicycle with a banana seat when I was ten, when all the cool girls had banana seats and I had to ride a bike with a dorky triangle seat instead. Before I die, I just want you to know that I still

---

[1] I only looked up anal bleaching because I was skeptical about its effectiveness!

haven't forgiven you for ruining my childhood" **#noregrets** (see "old ass" and look for the term "hashtag").

Having these conversations can be hard at first, but I've found that if I start from a place of victimhood, it gets easier. I visualize all those times I felt like I got fucked over, which enables me to come up with all the hostile words I need to find closure with my ~~perpetrators and offenders~~ family and friends. I also keep careful records of my emotions. Whenever a particular feeling of bitter resentment comes over me, I jot it down in a notepad, along with the name of the wrongdoer, so I don't forget. (You never know who you're going to run into. It's good to be prepared.)

For me, these honest, heart-to-heart talks are akin to an emotional cleanse.[2] It's all very healing. Well ... for me, anyway. (I'd never be so forward as to speak for the other participants.)

Of course, your results may vary. In fact, I should add a general disclaimer: The advice offered herein is dubious at best. You probably shouldn't heed any of it, but if you do, I'm not responsible for the results. (Unless your results are excellent, in which case, you're welcome.) If you decide not to do any confronting, you may wish to consider journaling, instead; after all, if loved ones read your journal *after* you're dead, they can hardly stay mad, can they? Incidentally, this is another advantage to having a terminal illness (which by definition has very few perks): You can be in an exceedingly shitty mood, fairly constantly, and no one will tell you off, because you're about to die. It's like having a license to bitch.

News of my impending death came in the form of some chilling results from a core needle biopsy of my left breast. (Stay tuned for

---

[2] And like any good cleanse, it must include vodka. I'm sure someone on the internet has already come up with a five-day, fruit-flavored vodka cleanse, and I love them for it.

the joys of the core needle biopsy procedure in a later chapter, which I hope to write before I die.)[3] My doctors had been closely "monitoring" my left boob for some years (which is to say, charging me large sums of money for doing nothing in particular) when my gynecologist felt a lump. She had me follow up with a sadistic boob-flattening procedure called a slammogram (or "diagnostic mammogram" if you want to get all technical about it). This abuse was immediately followed by an ultrasound, which evidently revealed something "suspicious."

I don't feel that I'm going out on a limb to say that if a radiologist tells you she sees something "suspicious" on a mammogram and ultrasound, she doesn't mean something benevolent, like a third nipple or a disappointed milk duct.[4] She probably means "suspicious" as in, *it looks like you have breast cancer.* She just won't come right out and say it. Radiologists like to punt on giving out bad news, preferring to let someone else field any particularly shitty balls. I felt like that one guy in every war movie who gets hit by enemy fire and becomes just a head and a torso, asking his friend (the radiologist, in my case), "Is it bad?" Then the friend always says something like, "It's going to be fine, just stay with me."

Spoiler alert: It's *never* fine.

The radiologist told me I needed to see a breast surgeon to undergo an invasive boob excavation. This would entail a biopsy of the horrific thing in my left tit, which was probably stage IV cancer, by shoving a humongous needle into it (or words to that effect). This particular form of boob torture is called a core needle biopsy.

---

[3] Just building suspense here. This book is like a fucking crime thriller already.

[4] My milk ducts, like my parents, are probably very disappointed that I never had kids.

After I got this procedure and they had my tissue sample (a long cylindrical section of my boob), it took over a week to get the results from my breast surgeon, whom we shall call Dr. Cutter. I tried to distract myself from all the anxious waiting by shopping online. I looked for different types of fashionable hats and scarves that might look good on my soon-to-be bald chemo-head. I also spent a good deal of time deliberating the pros and cons of "paint on" eyebrows. I decided against (couldn't find the right color).

I figured I should try to do some reading to get my mind off my worries, so I reread Dr. Elizabeth Kubler-Ross's book, *On Death and Dying*. I wondered how quickly I might get to the "acceptance stage" of the five stages of dying, since I was still stuck in the "why me" stage. (Why hadn't serial killers, military despots, pedophiles, or my greedy former boss gotten cancer instead of me? Not that I wish cancer on anyone—I'm just saying, if I had to pick someone to give cancer to, it wouldn't be me.)

I was soon at the point where I was trying to determine where in my living room I should place the hospital bed in which I'd die. The ideal placement would give me a clear view of the TV, with room for a mini-fridge next to it—but I was still undecided between a portable commode or a bedpan. On the one hand, a bedpan could easily be slid under my ass so I'd never have to get up. On the other hand, ew. I asked my husband, Fran, if he had any suggestions—he'd be the one emptying it, after all—but he kept reminding me that the biopsy was a precaution and I should try to relax and not worry so much. So *I* had to remind *him* about how breast cancer is the second leading cause of death among women (I googled this factoid, just to throw it in his face), and how the *first* leading cause of death among *men* was telling their wives to relax (I made up this factoid, just to throw it in his face), and how when I inevitably died from breast cancer (probably tomorrow), he'd feel terrible about it.

While Fran explained that we didn't know for sure, yet, whether or not I *had* cancer, I began jotting down notes for my funeral arrangements. I was thinking a single Scottish bagpiper to play "Amazing Grace," but also "O Sole Mio" for the Italian relatives, and "Hava Nagila," for the Jewish side of the family—wanting to keep things light, of course. My funeral would be a celebration of a life well lived. Well, a life lived, in any case. I also wanted to be buried next to Princess Diana, on the little island at Althorp. (This is more for you than for me, Fran. I'm sure you want a place where you can mourn in peace, when you visit me, daily.)

Waiting for biopsy results is especially horrid for someone who has anxiety issues and on-again, off-again (mostly on-again) insomnia. I spent a ridiculous amount of time lying awake every night, hyper-focusing on every twinge in my boob, certain I could feel the cancer spreading. I'd work myself into a panic and weep like a teen with a huge zit on her chin right before prom, like it was the end of the world. (On the plus side, facing my own mortality at four in the morning took my mind off not being able to sleep.)

Finally, though, my wait was over. Dr. Cutter called to give me the results. The call went something like this:

DR. CUTTER: I'm terribly sorry, Mrs. McCool, but I'm afraid the news isn't good. You have very invasive breast cancer.

ME: (Choking back a sob.) Oh my gawd ... has it reached stage IV already?

DR. CUTTER: I'm afraid you're at stage MCMLXVIII. Honestly, I was a little surprised when you answered the phone.

ME: (Remaining silent, trying to process the news.)

DR. CUTTER: Are you still there, Mrs. McCool?

ME: (Finally breaking my silence.) Yes.

DR. CUTTER: Wow.

Well, that's what it sounded like when she told me the lab had found lobular carcinoma in situ (LCIS) and atypical ductile hyperplasia (ADH) cells in the tissue sample. Both of these cell types are cancer indicators (often found in the company of cancer cells), and ADH is also considered to be a pre-cancerous condition (and should be removed), so she wanted to do another, larger biopsy as soon as possible.

Granted, I'm no Latin scholar, but "carcinoma" sounds a whole lot like a fancy word for cancer. Well, *pedicabo*[5] me, I had a pre-cancerous lesion. I thought I had prepared myself to hear the surgeon say they found breast cancer, and I had also been feeling the teensiest bit self-assured about my ability to deal with that diagnosis. I imagined I'd be all *Tuesdays with Morrie* about it ... giving advice from my deathbed to my niece and nephew, who would go on to write Pulitzer Prize–winning books about all the brilliant life lessons I taught them. But in the back of my mind, I had never acknowledged that it might actually come to that. Cancer happens to *other* people, not me. When you hear **the c-word** (see "old ass") used in reference to a boob that happens to be attached to *you*, it is insanely scary, and no! Not *that* c-word, the *other* c-word. The one that stands for cancer, **FFS** (see "old ass").

When the surgeon told me all this, I shrieked and told her the lab guy was a fucking idiot and made a mistake, and could she go

---

[5] I'm hoping "pedicabo me" means "fuck me" in Latin. If it doesn't, blame the Google translator. It could mean "just as I predicted," or "take me to Cabo," or "I want a pediatrician," which, come to think of it, all sound like things I might say after learning I have a pre-cancerous lesion.

back and check the tissue sample again, please, oh please, oh please? Or, at least, that's what I told her in my head. What I actually said was, "Uhhh ... so, what now?"

The procedure Dr. Cutter wanted to do next was called a wire localization breast biopsy. I peed a little. She must have thought I wouldn't know what a wire localization breast biopsy was (I didn't) and used that term thinking it sounded better than "lumpectomy" (it does). Frankly, any word ending in *-ectomy*, or even *-otomy*, sounds unpleasant, which is presumably why she avoided them. The surgeon then transferred me to her assistant so I could schedule the day on which I wanted to die on the operating table during a lumpectomy.

I handled this with a great deal of aplomb, if I say so myself. The secretary got on the line and asked, "So, Mrs. McCool, I understand we need to schedule you for a wire localization biopsy in the hospital?"

In a high-pitched voice only my dogs could hear, I said, "No! Please don't let her cut my left tit off!" Then I coughed quickly, gathered myself, unmuted the phone, and replied, "Why yes, how's next Thursday?" I bet she never even noticed my discomfort.[6]

I hung up and promptly freaked out. I should explain what I mean when I say I "freaked out," as every person likely has a different definition of the phrase. For example, a pre-teen girl might say she "freaked out" when her friend got her a ticket to a **Justin Bieber** (see "old ass") concert. I mean the polar opposite of that. To make things clearer, have a look at the chart below, which represents my varying levels of anxiety.

---

[6] She probably did notice my discomfort, because at this point, my voice became high and trembly—very similar in pitch and resonance to that of Minnie Mouse sitting atop a washing machine set to agitate.

My Typical Anxiety Levels on a Scale from 1 to 10

(with apologies to Edvard Munch)

Anxiety Level 1	Anxiety Level 2.5	Anxiety Level 5	Anxiety Level 7.5	Anxiety Level 10
Asleep or too drunk to give any shits	Concerned but not terribly worried	A bit anxious about some vague threat	Uptight and unprepared for impending doom	Full-blown, batshit-crazy panic attack

Level 1 is pretty self-explanatory. It's hard to get all worked up with anxiety when you're sleeping or really drunk, so at Level 1, let's say I'm nearly unruffled. At level 2.5, I might be wondering if there is possibly an escaped prisoner in our area, and I'm kicking myself for watching *Roseanne* reruns instead of the news. A violent fugitive nearby is troubling, but a martini and a sitcom could fairly easily distract me from dwelling on it.[7]

At Level 5, I am now almost certain there is an escaped killer in my immediate area, specifically because it would be just my bleeding luck that the one night I didn't watch the local news, I missed the escaped-violent-convict segment. This level is roughly normal for me. While it certainly warrants an increase on the worrisome scale, I

---

[7] I should have made this a scale from 1 to 5, since I only drew 5 faces, but having already committed to using a scale from 1 to 10, we're stuck with the ridiculous and uneven levels of 2.5 and 7.5, because now it's a fucking math problem.

could still, possibly, be diverted from focusing on my fears by two martinis and a particularly funny episode of *Mike & Molly*.[8]

At level 7.5, I'm becoming terribly uncomfortable with the way things have progressed, as the murderer is now undoubtedly within a one-mile radius of my house. Fran's already asleep in bed, and although I need to lock the sliding doors before I go upstairs, I'm afraid the deranged serial killer will be waiting right outside for me to get close enough to the door so he can grab me and pull me outside where Fran won't hear my screams. I'm in a frightening quandary: A Xanax would probably be effective in distracting me, but I've already had four martinis, so taking one is out of the question.

My only hope is a fifth martini.

At anxiety Level 10, I'm in the bathroom, peeing (after five or seven martinis, depending on the current threat level), when it dawns on me that while I was in the bathroom, the deranged serial killer guy probably snuck in through the unlocked sliding doors, killed Fran and the dogs, and is waiting right outside the bathroom door to kill me next. Also, like an idiot, I forgot to bring my cell phone into the bathroom, so I can't call 911 just when I'm about to be raped and have my liver eaten with a nice Chianti. I try to come up with a plan to sneak past the psycho rapist serial killer cannibal so I can make a ninth martini to calm my nerves, but my planning skills are, by now, somewhat dubious. At first, I'm pumped up about "the plan," but eventually I have to admit that after eleventy martinis, there's no way I'm gonna be able to do a somersault, let alone a

---

[8] *Mike & Molly* is a hilarious sitcom starring Melissa McCarthy and some other people whose names I forget and it doesn't matter because MELISSA McCARTHY! I love to condescendingly make fun of Molly's (Melissa's) sister Victoria, who is always stoned, while sitting on my couch drinking vodka. Stupid potheads. They always say the thumbest dings *hiccup*.

round-house kick to the killer's groin. I decide I should remain in the bathroom. I think I read somewhere that humans can survive for more than three weeks on water alone. By that time, surely the psychopath will have grown bored (and hungry) and gone looking for another victim.

So getting back to my boob story ... *after* I got off the phone with my breast surgeon, I googled everything she told me. In addition to learning that Google is *not* my friend, my anxiety level shot right to 11. *That's* what I mean when I say I "freaked out," and yes, I realize choosing the number 11 on a scale of 1 to 10 is only slightly less annoying than when someone asks for a 110% effort, which is why I didn't say my anxiety level was DEFCON 24. Because I *never* exaggerate.[9]

When I heard I needed more surgery, I was aghast.[10] I closely resembled a man who had just suffered a roundhouse kick to the bojangles by a drunken woman who somersaulted out of a bathroom. I became equal parts shocked and horrified.

I tried to calm myself down a bit before I called my parents, who were, naturally, waiting for news. I took a deep breath and dialed their number. Dad picked up, but before I could actually tell him what the doctor said, I started bawling and hung up. I never asked, but I bet I made him shit himself. Wouldn't have been the first time, and probably won't be the last. Sorry, Dad. (And some people wonder why I never had kids—it's because they do crap like this to you over the phone!)

---

[9] Saying I *never* exaggerate might be a bit of an exaggeration. (DEFCON 24, however, is not.)

[10] This is a *massive* understatement. It's the Everest of understatements. It makes all the other understatements embarrassed about calling themselves understatements, and leaves them feeling like gently rolling hills within spitting distance of slight exaggeration.

But I'm getting ahead of myself. I should really go back to the beginning of my story, back to when and how this cancer-scare nightmare truly started. (By the way, this is an old storyteller trick, where you get the reader hooked and, in the middle of the really exciting part, you bring the narrative to a screeching halt, and do a flashback of all the less dramatic shit that led up to it, because storytellers can be dicks.)

At this very point, I'm sure you're all **OMG** (see "old ass"), what the hell happened next? You may be asking yourself certain questions—or, if you aren't, here are some questions you *could* ask yourself: Does Karen indeed have invasive breast cancer? Does she go through with the lumpectomy, or does she brashly refuse to have her breast mutilated and decide, instead, to fight her cancer with holistic methods she learned about on How_To_Kill_Cancer_By_Eating_Only_Beets_for_24_Days.com?[11] Did the beet diet cure her? Or maybe it *would* have cured her but she died anyway when she started shitting red and thought the cancer had spread to her colon? (Cause of death: fright.)

Or, did Karen go through with the surgery, but the surgeon operated on the *wrong* breast, and the lingering cancer spread quickly? But then! What if Karen stumbled on an ancient Aztec script that mysteriously showed up in a borrowed library book with some oxymoronic title like, *How to Die Well,* that included a map to a rare plant root that, when used as a suppository, cures cancer ... like the fuckin' *Da Vinci Code* for boobs? (Eventual cause of death: crushed by a pile of money earned from royalties on sales of blockbuster cancer thriller.)

Or ... omigod ... what if the surgeon was drunk, slipped with

---

[11] I don't know if this is a real website or not. If it is, a) I am in no way affiliated with this it, and b) OMG, that's hilarious!

the scalpel, removed both breasts, and nicked Karen's heart in the process? (Cause of death: incompetence of surgeon who operated while on day four of a five-day fruit-flavored vodka cleanse.) Or maybe Karen died on the operating table, but got "sent back" (surely it wasn't her time yet? She had a book to finish, after all) and mercifully, after her near-death experience, she no longer feared death and took a trip to Disney World with all the money she saved on bras and Xanax.

Of course, things may have taken a dark turn: Karen maybe decided not to "go back" (fuck the book; the afterlife is probably pretty amazing) and died during the lumpectomy. And maybe the horrible details of the surgeon's ineptitude came to light only after one nurse went all *Silkwood*[12] on the hospital's ass. Then the nurse probably died in a suspicious car accident, and the TV series of this book will have a spin-off documentary on Netflix about the nurse's assassination at the hands of the corrupt hospital administration. (God bless the whistle-blower for providing another royalty stream to Karen's heirs.)

Crap—can you believe both a nurse and I died after a "routine" breast biopsy? You may think all this sounds pretty fanciful, but it's nothing compared to all the horrifying scenarios that came to my mind during the days leading up to my lumpectomy. (I excel at coming up with worst-case scenarios. It's one of my supah powahs.)

I did warn you this was going to be a harrowing tale, didn't I?

---

[12] *Silkwood* was a movie, starring Meryl Streep, about an activist named Karen Silkwood, who uncovered dangerous working conditions at the nuclear facility where she was employed. Karen was supposedly killed in a car accident (although some suspect that she was murdered by her employers for her activism). I am using the word Silkwood here as an adjective, because that's a new way we've bastardized the English language. We use nouns as adjectives now. We're all doomed.

(There is a strong warning in the addendum, in case you missed it.)

Some people may be thinking, "Well, she certainly doesn't die. She wrote this book, after all."

I've got two words for those fucking know-it-alls: "finished posthumously." It's also entirely possible I had the foresight to start writing this book waaaay before I died and Fran finished it for me (he's thoughtful like that; I can't even remember the last time he left the toilet seat up) to ensure the world benefits from my written legacy.[13] That's right—'cause I'm a legacy-leaver. We're like job creators, only real. We legacy-leavers like to make the world a better place by passing on all the wisdom we've accumulated. Because sharing is caring (unless it's gonorrhea).

This book, my most recent legacy project, chronicles the lessons I learned about how to die with grace and humility. It's going to be the best book about life ever. I'm writing it for all the future generations. (You're very welcome, future generations.) My other legacy project involves using macaroni art and finger painting to work on your shame and self-loathing, but that will be an instructional video.

I just had a sad thought. Will future generations even *be* readers? Fran, you need to make this into an audiobook. Oh fuck right off. I can't believe you aren't going to make this into an audiobook! You would deny illiterate or lazy folks the enjoyment of a tragically beautiful yet uplifting cancer story? Not to be a selfish dick, but I don't have the time to do it myself, 'cause I'm dying of cancer. This world needs more compassion. And audiobooks by legacy-leavers. Just sayin'. Someone call Susan Sarandon. She'd probably do it. She's got a great voice and she's a humanitarian who gives a shit.

---

[13] Okay, while *possible* I had the foresight to finish writing before I died, it's highly implausible, if I'm being honest. Too often, I don't even have enough foresight to check the level of toilet paper remaining before I take a shit.

You know what? Maybe just go right to making a blockbuster movie. Get Spielberg to executive produce it and add something about a new dinosaur that was genetically engineered from my breast tissue (a Ptittydactyl?). That way even young people who don't read can benefit from my wisdom.

I'm sure I'll get invited to do a **TED talk** (see "old ass"), but I won't be able to, because, thankfully, I'll be dead. (I hate public speaking.) I'm going to use "being dead" as my excuse to get out of all public appearances. Barnes & Noble will call me and ask if I can speak at their flagship store in Manhattan, and I'll be like, "Can't. I'll be dead." Then they'll stock the shit out of my book, and promote the hell out of it, because a dead author means the work sells at a premium.

You know, we could go with a TV mini-series. I'd like either Melissa McCarthy or Mamrie Hart[14] to play me. Shit, I can't believe I won't be alive to see it. By the way, this is officially my dying wish, so you have to do it now, Lorne Michaels. Don't be a douche.

My apologies, in advance, to whoever gets cast to play the role of me, but I know that either of you (Melissa or Mamrie) will easily bounce back from this dreadful, critic-panned series. Sure, they'll say the story and dialogue were horrendous, and yes, they'll say the character of Karen was totally unlikeable, unsympathetic, and a complete numpty, but when they see you nail that scene with the paper cup on your boob, you'll be up for an Emmy. I pinky swear. (Sorry for the unannounced spoiler, but I can't wait until you get to the part in the story where I have a paper cup taped to my boob before surgery.

---

[14] Mamrie Hart is a YouTuber, author, actor, screenwriter, and a helluva mixologist. Her YouTube channel is called "You Deserve a Drink." (And I do! I really, really do.) She's hilarious.

It's so un-fucking-believable. You're going to love it. See drawing below.)

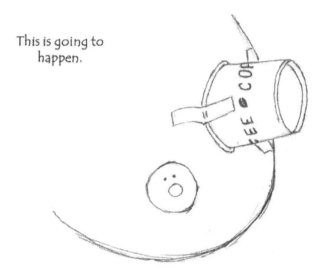

This is going to happen.

Most critics are fussy old white men, anyway. The kind of bourgeois assclowns who call movies "films." (I'm only sayin' what everyone's thinkin'.) Like, take Philly film critic, Patrick Stoner—that great big goodie-goodie movie-nerd (with the incredibly ironic last name). He can kiss my dead fat ass if he bad-mouths the series. What would these guys know about the terror of a woman's struggle with breast cancer and how hard it is to write a good made-for-TV screenplay about it? Nothing, that's what.

Or, even harder, to write a book. I'm sure screenplays are challenging to write and all, but let's face it, writing a book is waaaay harder. For a screenplay you only have to adapt the *already written* book. Pfft ... how hard can *that* be?

Now that I've pissed off *every* screenwriter, maybe I should write my *own* screenplay of this book. Shouldn't leave anything to chance when you're dying ... or risk a shitty adaptation. Naturally, the movie will make extensive use of the voice-over (so the audience can hear my every unsettling thought), but will include lots of cuts to my wacky daydreams, like on *Scrubs*, to keep the mood light. A dramedy like *M*A*S*H*, only with more trauma. Of course, this all depends on how long I live with what is probably very invasive breast cancer. I'm guessing six to eight weeks, at the outside. Is that enough time to finish a book *and* a screenplay? I need to stock up on martinis. My plan is to die very drunk, under suspicious circumstances, which I think should improve book sales.

First things first, though: finish the book. Need. To. Finish. This. Book. Let's get right down to it then. Have to stay focused. Roll up the ol' sleeves. Start crackin'.

* * *

All right—I'm going to start cracking in a couple of minutes, but first, it's time for a short break. I need to pop into the kitchen and get myself another glass of iced green tea, because it's hot as hell outside and writing in a lounge chair on a deck is reaaally exhausting. (I should be more concerned about sunblock than writer's block, but at this point, getting skin cancer is the least of my worries.) Plus, I'm pissed off at Patrick Stoner for panning my mini-series, so I'm feeling a little peeved, and it's throwing off my concentration.

* * *

I'm back, but before I pick up with the story again ... I've got a question: Who here likes long chapters? Anyone? No hands. *I know*. I really hate long chapters, too. All right, that's settled. There's only one thing I'd like to leave you with, and that is a tantalizing cliff-hanger.

Unfortunately, I don't have a tantalizing cliffhanger.

Chapter 2

Lessons in neurosis, the titty twister, and the end of the world

MY FIRST BOOB-RELATED HEALTH scare began a few years earlier with a wonky mammogram. There had been a "shadow" on some prior images that my doctors were "watching" (ignoring). Accordingly, I had a six-month follow-up mammogram two days before Thanksgiving. My boobs were manhandled, and I went home, feeling more than a little pleased to have gotten through my biannual titty torture without crying or shitting myself.[15] Unfortunately, my relief was short-lived. I got a call from the radiology office the next day, saying they needed to take more images.[16]

If I had to summarize my feelings in only three words, they would be: Fan. Fuckin'. Tastic.

---

[15] To avoid confusion, I'd like the record to state that I've never actually soiled myself during a mammogram. I'm using the phrase "shitting myself" as a metaphor for being incredibly anxious.

[16] This is the point at which I shat. (This is not a metaphor.)

And really? Is this what we're doing now? Twice-weekly mammograms? What's next? I go in every morning and come back again after lunch? Should I just bring my bathrobe and a toothbrush to keep at your place, Mr. Radiologist? Cheesus.

By the by: Did you know that you can get radiation-induced breast cancer from mammograms? Just a fun fact I picked up.

I was worried about why they needed more images. Most women would probably tell you mammograms aren't a big deal, and they're (mostly) right. But for a person who suffers from anxiety (moi), *all* medical procedures are distressing. If I needed surgery for a bunion, I'd be worried the doctor would slip and I'd lose a couple of toes. And, of course, it'd be my big toe and the one next to it, so there'd be nothing to keep my flip-flops on. I'd have to drag my foot around, so my "flop" wouldn't fall off, and because of my shuffle-walk, children would start calling me the "three-toed zombie freak." Then one of those doomsday preppers who takes *The Walking Dead*[17] waaay too seriously would shoot me in the head with a crossbow.

So you can see how even a "minor" surgery can lead to my tragic death.

These irrational fears (and my mind's tendency to exaggerate them) could be, in part, because when I was little, my dad would warn us kids about all the ways we could "poke an eye out." (Incidentally, these warnings are also one of the reasons why my brothers and I found the movie *A Christmas Story* so hilariously/sadly relatable.) To Dad, "horsing around" was one of the most perilous activities one could engage in (that, and not looking both ways when

---

[17] *The Walking Dead* is a TV show about the zombie apocalypse. It's kind of like what you'd get if you made a show about Donald Trump's dystopic version of America and then added a bunch of dead people. If you've got a bad ticker, don't watch this show without having a defibrillator handy.

crossing the street). Dad seemed to know a disturbing number of people who knew people who had lost an eye by horsing around. He was evangelical about pointy things maintaining safe distances from defenseless eyeballs, and boy could he preach. I once had my cheek scratched by our kitten and I thought Dad's sermon was never going to end. He was like a sanctimonious priest, warning about eternal damnation in the fires of hell. Dad really put the *Father* in *fatherhood.*

During my childhood, Dad had a constantly growing list of Things You Don't Want to Lose. By the time I was a teenager, the list looked something like this:

Dad's List of Things You Don't Want to Lose

1) Your hearing

2) Your teeth

3) An eye

4) A finger (added after one of my brothers accidentally shut a car door on my hand)

5) Your homework, which you probably left in your locker again, and why are you just starting this project when it's due tomorrow

6) Your virginity

And on it went....

When we were really little, Dad's lectures would go something like this: "Did you remember to brush your teeth? You don't want to lose all your teeth, do you? You'll end up talking like Toothless Tom."

He'd say all this with his lips rolled over his teeth, so the word toothless was pronounced "toofleth," and he'd pretend-smack his toothless gums together after each sentence, while whistling all his *s*'s.

Once we became teenagers, his lectures got more serious: "Turn that music down! You don't want to lose your hearing, do you?"

The lectures also grew more dramatic, and the slippery slopes got slipperier: "If you're not home by 11:30, you'll end up getting pregnant. Then you'll drop out of school and have to flip burgers for the rest of your life. Do you want to flip burgers the rest of your life? No, you don't, because you'll become an alcoholic and end up in jail or living in a gutter. And that's if you don't overdose on heroin first! Do you want to OD on heroin? No? Then you better be home by 11:30."

If missing a curfew can lead to pregnancy and heroin addiction, it's not hard to envision how a simple medical procedure could lead to my early demise.

My dad's warnings about serious bodily harm may have played a part in my being such a namby-pamby when it comes to medical stuff, but I also inherited "white coat syndrome" from my mom. She's a carrier. I'm sure she got it from her mom, and it probably goes back generations to the very first Scottish woman who went to some quack-druid-priest-witch-doctor guy who thought drilling a hole in her head would cure her of "the bad vapours" that caused urinary tract infections, then told her to avoid drinking cranberry juice and charged her two live chickens.

Mom had always been afraid of doctors and dentists.[18] One of her excuses for not going to the doctor was that she knew lots of people in their eighties who hadn't seen a doctor in sixty years, and they were all perfectly healthy. None of these octogenarians had ever had a colonoscopy, and not one of them got colon cancer. *Ipso facto,* avoiding colonoscopies leads to healthy colons. I'm leaning toward her being right on this one. (I don't want a colonoscopy, either.)

I think maybe a few people in my mom's family believed there was a strong, positive correlation between going to a doctor and getting ill—like you can't catch cancer if you never go to the doctor. Maybe it's a Scottish thing? I can imagine a group of old ladies in my mom's hometown of Kirkintilloch trying to one-up each other on how long it's been since they'd last seen a doctor: "Yoo went fuhrrty year ago, ye say? Och, no, I haevna been since my Archie were jes a wee laddie, and he's noo sexty-sex. And reet I was not tae hae gone; I ne'wer had aught but a sniffle."[19]

It's like they think if you've never gone to a doctor, it's pretty safe for you to share a sippy cup with an Ebola patient.

Bottom line: My mom was afraid of going to the doctor, and so am I, because you should always listen to your mother. So, between Dad's worries about permanent bodily injury and Mom's fear of doctors, I came by my own anxieties honestly enough. (If we were in the Cone of Silence,[20] I'd confess I'm trying to blame my crazy on

---

[18] I should clarify that this has changed recently. After my mom fell, she seems to have lost her fear of doctors and dentists. I guess after you break an arm and a hip, nothing can scare you anymore.

[19] Translation: "You went forty years ago, you say? Oh, no, I haven't been since my Archie was just a little boy, and he's now sixty-six. And right I was not to have gone; I never had anything but a sniffle."

[20] If you were born after the sixties and never watched reruns of the sitcom *Get Smart,* sorry about that, Chief. You missed it by *that* much.

my parents, instead of admitting to being a self-taught hot mess, but in case they're listening, it's all their fault.)

I don't worry about my health on a daily basis, mind you. I'm not one of those hypochondriacs who goes to **WebMD** (see "old ass") every other week with some new, imagined disorder. But I feel like when I have a legitimate health scare (e.g., a wonky mammogram), I should be allowed to worry. And I do—I worry *hard!* Work hard, worry hard. That's my motto. (Note to self: Get a new motto.) When I had an "abnormal" pap smear in my mid-twenties, I worried about cervical cancer *like it was my job.*

So when the radiologist's office called to say they needed more mammogram images, I was scared, because *hello!* They must have seen something ominous. (Cue the theme song from *Jaws. Dun dun. Dun dun. Dun dun dun dun dun dun dun dun.*) Fuck me. I was upset and petrified, but I was also terribly annoyed that I needed to make a second trip. Goddammit. I started wondering, "Who fucked up and didn't finish the job yesterday? Did the technician forget to put film in the machine? Did the radiologist spill his mocha double latte all over the originals? Was it because I had my eyes closed? Because the technician never told me I had to keep my eyes open."

I was getting more and more pissed, so I told the secretary, in no uncertain terms, "Oh ... of course ... no problem at all. I can come in tomorrow, if that's good for you?"

The next day, being Thanksgiving, wasn't good for them (lazy fuckers). Nor was Friday, Saturday, Sunday, or Monday (uncaring bastards), so I had to spend the entire freaking weekend being desperately worried about my left tit. Not the most relaxing way to spend a holiday. I was going to be livid if it turned out I had cancer that could have been cured had I started chemo on Thursday, but since they made me wait until Tuesday, I got sent straight to hospice. That would have really chapped my ass.

Lest you think I *am* a hypochondriac in denial, I have plenty of reasons for getting worked up over a simple mammogram (read: following are a bunch of excuses for all my drama). My mom was given a drug called DES (diethylstilbestrol) when she was pregnant with me to (allegedly) prevent a miscarriage. Um, yeah ... what could *possibly* go wrong with prescribing synthetic estrogen to pregnant women? Turns out DES causes cancer. (There's a shocker.) We'll talk more about DES later, but goddammit, Doc, what the actual fuck?

I also blame pharmaceutical companies and their massive ad campaigns. They market drugs for every conceivable ailment, and they rarely invent a drug you have to take only once. Usually, it's four times a day for the rest of your life, and it costs more monthly than the gross national product of Zimbabwe. Big Pharma has developed a drug for every imaginable first-world medical problem. They even started (purportedly) making up disorders. For example, when Eli Lilly's patent ran out on the antidepressant, Prozac, they got a new patent and rebranded it under the fresher, more feminine-sounding name of Sarafem. They then marketed it to women to treat menstrual symptoms, including severe mood swings. The powers-that-be called this new disease Premenstrual Dysphoric Disorder (PMDD).[21]

Some medical folks are like, "Ummm... thaaaat doesn't sound like a thing."

I'm not a doctor, but seriously, many researchers and physicians are debating whether or not PMDD is a real disorder. Yet treating this perhaps overly diagnosed disorder seems to be very profitable. According to the American Psychological Association website,

---

[21] See: http://www.drugwatch.com/2012/01/22/disease-mongering-and-drug-marketing

Eli Lilly spent over $33 million in advertising for Sarafem. Within the first seven months of approval, physicians wrote over 200,000 prescriptions for it.[22]

Isn't it awesome how doctors were suddenly able to diagnose PMDD in their patients and sell them the Sarafem cure? Downright magical. Of course, PMDD may indeed be a real thing, and if it is, Eli Lilly had better hope the women who have it don't start comparing the price difference between Prozac and Sarafem (Prozac costs less), or the drug company is going to have some splainin' to do to some very stabby women.

A quick Google search on the cost of Sarafem reveals the price to be, apparently, anywhere from $300 to just under $500 for thirty tablets. If each prescription was for thirty tablets, it means that, in the first seven months alone, Eli Lilly would have made ... well, let's just say they would have made enough money to buy a senator with enough left over to give Dr. Oz an endorsement deal.

So, great. Pharmaceutical companies spend millions on advertising drugs—some of which are for controversial disorders—instead of investing in research that might, oh, I don't know ... be a tad more worthwhile, like, say, in *preventing cancer*?! In the case of DES, Big Pharma came up with a drug to prevent miscarriages that doesn't actually prevent miscarriages, but it does *cause cancer*. Well done, pharmaceutical companies. You dicks.

Do I sound bitter? Maybe it's because I can't turn on the TV without being bombarded with commercials for treatments for everything from <u>a</u>nal leakage to <u>z</u>its. There are drugs for dry eyes, watery eyes, oily skin, dry skin, sleeplessness, staying awake, inability to pee, peeing too much, having the shits, not being able to shit ... and you

---

[22] See: http://www.apa.org/monitor/oct02/pmdd.aspx

can't flip through the channels without coming across an infomercial for some new miracle drug that'll help you "Drop the pounds!" while you sit on your fat ass eating fast food and ice cream (and as a side note, this must seriously make world hunger organizations want to punch themselves in the face).

But we all fall for it! Those fucking commercials work. And some doctors take kickbacks for prescribing certain drugs. (You can find public records here: https://openpaymentsdata.cms.gov/)

Why should doctors advise restless patients—who drink waaaaay too many Red Bulls or grande double-caffeinated lattes—to simply give up caffeine, when it's far more lucrative to diagnose ADHD? That way, the doctor can bill people every six months for an office visit to write another refill for Ritalin.

Speaking of doctor visits, I've noticed my doctors *hate* it when I try to talk about two issues during the same visit. For example, I once went to a doctor because I had a terrible sinus infection. I asked, "While I'm here, do you think you could also refill my prescription for Xanax?"

He rolled his eyes so hard I thought he was having a seizure. He said, "I'll do it this time, but you need to make a separate appointment for that in the future."

He was all exasperated, as if I was asking him to do me some huge favor, like drive me to the airport or help me to assemble a dining room set from Ikea. Then he wrote a prescription for a measly fifteen pills, which took him all of two seconds, and I'm sure he threw this hissy fit because he couldn't bill my insurance company for two visits.

My doctors do this all the time now. They won't discuss two

different issues in one visit. It's always, "We need to schedule another appointment to go over that."[23]

Is it just me or is this seriously fucked up?

Anyway, back to my point: So my mom was given DES while pregnant. The good news: DES apparently prevented a miscarriage, in my case.[24] How fabulous for me! The bad news: In utero exposure to DES greatly increases the risk of cervical, breast, vaginal, uterine, ovarian, and testicular cancers in the offspring. How fucking fantastic. (Silver lining: Only my older brother has to worry about testicular cancer. I dodged *that* bullet.)[25]

I had a scare with cervical cancer in my late twenties, and I had surgery that we'll talk about later, but since then, I haven't had any more frightening Pap smear results. So cervical cancer hasn't killed me (yet), but breast cancer is a new concern, especially since I'm over forty, which is when DES seems to change its main focus from the vag area to the boobs. All of my lady-parts are now officially trying to kill me.

---

[23] And before you say it, no, it's not because I'm one of those patients who wants to stay in the exam room kvetching for an hour. I always want to get the fuck out of there as quickly as possible.

[24] But did it? Did it, really? It could be like that old joke about the man guarding his property from elephants by sitting on his porch with an elephant gun. A neighbor asks him, "Why? There aren't any elephants around here." "See," says the old man. "It works."

[25] Note: My friend and editor Lola pointed out that this seemed like a good place for a joke about balls, which is complete bollocks. She's obviously a little nuts. Lost her marbles, if you will. I see you groin tired of this, Lola, but #CantStopWontStop, #SorryNotSorry. I've got some cojones saying all this, since I know you'll be editing it ... but Lola, don't get all teste with me ... this clearly isn't the place for silly jokes about testicles, even if it is low-hanging fruit. #NailedIt #HeyOh.

The first time I had an ultrasound on a lump in my breast, I was so scared that I cried during the procedure. At one point, when the technician paused with the probe/wand in one spot for more than a few seconds, I thought for sure she was about to tell me that she saw an enormous tumor. I expected her to turn the screen toward me so we could both watch as it spread to my brain.

Really. I cried. It wasn't like I was bawling loudly and sucking in my lower lip or anything (because *I* am an adult), so thankfully, the technician never even noticed. (It was very nice of the technician to pretend like she didn't notice. Health-care techs can be incredibly kind. Except when they're fucking up your mammogram images and making you come back for more! Gah!)

Anyhoo, after scheduling my follow-up mammogram, I decided to "celebrate" (wallow in my misery) by mixing myself a big-assed cocktail, because, *I know*, right? Say whaaat? Who's raising the roof? I am! I figured having a craptastic hangover on Thanksgiving Day would be totally tits.[26] And sadly, there I go again: I said tits. I'd become obsessed with them. I couldn't stop thinking about mine that entire holiday weekend—specifically, my left boob, which had gotten a callback (and not the good kind).

By Monday, I was telling myself, "Don't worry, Karen. Tomorrow you'll laugh at how much you were freaking out all weekend."

Then I went back to grumbling, "Oh, tomorrow, why aren't you here yet?"

---

[26] In case you didn't know, "tits" is slang for "spectacular" or "awesome." No, I don't know why, either. Your guess is as good as mine, but my working theory is this term was first coined by an adolescent boy conflating all things fabulous with boobies, and others agreed.

That's when I decided to take a Xanax. "Well, hellooooooo, helpful little pinkish-colored friend! Do you go well with big-assed cocktails? OMG! Me, too!"

Oh fer the love of Christ and all the saints, Fran, quit freaking out (and maybe you should stop reading this). Taking a Xanax with one drink (okay, two ... I'm not gonna lie) never killed anybody. Or maybe it did, but my point is, I was fine. Plus, the Xanax bottle said to "avoid" alcohol ... which is just a suggestion, really. It's not like it said "DO NOT DRINK ALCOHOL WHEN TAKING THIS MEDICATION," because if it had screamed at me in all caps like that, I wouldn't have taken it.

I went back for the second slammogram that Tuesday. First, they took about six images, and let's expound on that for just a moment: When I say they "took images," this wasn't an innocuous "hold still and say cheese" kind of thing. They flattened the shit out of my boob until I saw Jesus. Until this procedure, I had *no idea* how far away from my body my nipple could travel. It looked like a cartoon boob getting hit with a sledgehammer. It made me mildly nauseated when I looked down, which, in hindsight, was pretty stupid. I did not need to see that. (Lesson learned.)

The technician explained that the radiologist wanted to get a better look at "something" in my boob that a routine mammogram wouldn't pick up, so she was doing what I think she called a "titty twister"—a.k.a. a "diagnostic mammogram"—I don't recall her exact words. In a routine mammogram, they take images from two different positions. In a diagnostic mammogram, they take many more boob-punishing views, from all sorts of ungodly angles. This appeared to be achieved by switching out the machine's normal clamping device for even ghastlier attachments. At one point, the technician was evidently trying to include skin from my back in the images. She stretched and pulled so hard on my left side that my skin started to rotate around my torso. By the time she was finished, my right tit was in my right armpit. Suffice it to say that the experience was significantly worse than a routine mammogram.

Every now and again, the technician would say to me, "There's going to be a little bit of pressure. Take a deep breath and hold still."

I wanted to give *her* a little bit of pressure—right in her face.

The song "Coconut," by Harry Nilsson, started running through my head:

> *You put the lime in the coconut, you drink 'em bot' up /*
> *Put the lime in the coconut, you drink 'em bot' up / Put*
> *the lime in the coconut, you drink 'em bot' up*

That's how torturous it was—as a distraction, I started singing a song in my head that has no end.[27] (I hope it was only in my head.)

When the technician was done taking eleventy gillion images, she sent me back into the half-naked-lady holding pen to wait for the radiologist's review. (When you go in for a mammogram, you start out in the general waiting room or the "off street" waiting room, for lack of a better phrase. Then you change into a hospital gown and go into yet another waiting room, which I call the "holding pen," because it reminds me of the place where animals are kept before going to slaughter.)

I think my radiologist made a wager with a colleague that he could make a boob so flat that the nipple would pop off (I bet they do shit like that, the jerks), because he sent me back into the titty torture chamber for a few more excruciating, boob-squashing pics.

On the way, I walked by what I assumed was the radiologist's

---

[27] If you now have this song stuck in your head, you're welcome and I'm sorry.

office—a darkened room where some dorky guy was looking at mammogram images on a monitor. I flipped him the finger. If he had turned around, I'd have turned it into a friendly wave, but he didn't. Because he was a self-absorbed asshole.

For the next few images, I kept my eyes tightly shut. Actually, my entire face was squeezed together, and I probably looked a lot like someone who was expecting to get blasted in the mug with a water pistol ... or a pie. That thought really pissed me off, because I didn't get to enjoy my pie on Thanksgiving. I was too fuckin' worried about my tit! I told myself that, on the way back, I'd give that radiologist a two-handed, double-middle-finger, see-sawing gesture, even if he did turn around. No one should come between a woman and her pie.

When the images were done, the technician sent me back to the holding pen as we waited to hear if the radiologist needed anything else—like, maybe he'd want to haul out an industrial laundry press next, because so far, my nipple remained (miraculously) attached.

As I was sitting in the holding pen, I was petrified that they might have spotted cancer. Not an unreasonable concern, given that this was my second mammogram in a week. That's not being super hypochondriac-y, is it? They certainly wouldn't have called me back just because they liked taking pictures of my boobs. (God, I hope that's not why they had me come back.)

Although what if that *was* why? Maybe all the people who had been feeling my left boob lately just really, *really* liked it. It's understandable. My left boob *is* the more attractive of the two. It's slightly larger than the right, which is a bit of an underachiever. Then I thought, what if the radiologist was actually a seventh-grade boy who loved looking at X-rays of boobies? I didn't get a very good look at him. He totally could have been a teenage deviant, getting off on boobie X-rays, for all I could tell. (I can't believe my hospital hired an adolescent perv as a radiologist.)

Finally, the technician came in to tell me that the deviant Doogie Howser thought he saw breast cancer, but wanted to wait and look at it again in six months, because by that time it would have metastasized, and then he'd know for sure that it was cancer.

Okay, that's not word for word. She said something about how what the radiologist saw were most probably "benign calcifications," but that he wanted me to come back again in six months, so they could check for any changes.

So they were finally done with me. I went to change into my clothes, and I noticed my boob had angry, red marks on it—the kind that might be left by a strong mechanical clamping device. And I could have sworn my left boob looked a bit droopy. (See drawing below.)

My Post-Mammogram Ta-tas*

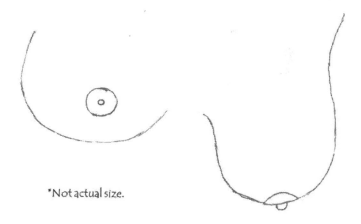

*Not actual size.

In fact, they'd basically deflated my boob until it looked like a Mylar helium balloon a few days after the party. I could have rolled it up like that witch's legs after a house fell on her.

I decided to show Fran when he got home from work.

ME: Do you want to see what they did to my boob today?

FRAN: Do I? (He said this with a lot less enthusiasm than I would have expected, given that I was about to show him my boobs. Undeterred, I lifted my shirt.)

ME: Look at this!

FRAN: You mean all the red marks?

ME: Yeah, the red marks ... but do you notice anything different?
(I was growing very impatient with his overt lack of interest in my tits. He shook his head and went to the fridge for a soda. Apparently, he *didn't* notice anything unusual. Now I was offended.)

ME: *Thanks*, Fran! I guess my left boob *always* looks deflated. Is that what you're telling me? Well, *that's* a little rude!

Fran exhaled, put back the soda, and reached for a beer.

I told Fran I had to go back (again!) in six months, then explained my theory that maybe all these people just liked touching my boobs. Fran coughed into his beer, and agreed this was very possible (good answer). I told him I was thinking I should start charging for it. He wasn't a fan of the idea. Maybe because he didn't want to have to start paying. Fran's very frugal.

Speaking of the name Fran, you may be thinking, *what's with her husband's name? Fran?* When I first heard his name, I was surprised, too. I was sure that was a girl's name. "Fran" is short for Francis, naturally. Well, I suppose I shouldn't say "naturally." It could also be short for Francisco. Or it could be really, *really* short for Fran-cobenebellabotto. But in his case, it's not.

I never cared for the name Fran. Apologies to my in-laws, whom I love dearly—and honest to God, my mother-in-law is so cute, if you ever met her you'd want to put her in your pocket and carry her around with you—but their taste in names is questionable.

Every Fran I ever met before my husband was a woman. But what's worse: Fran's a junior. *A junior!* Let's be honest ... *nobody* wants to be a junior. It confuses things, and naming kids after family members makes your family tree look weird.

And if you think about it, there are very few IIIs, which should be a clue. Of course, if your father or grandfather was incredibly famous, you'd definitely want to be a third. Like if my umpteenth great grandfather had been Abraham Lincoln, I'd totally have wanted to be named after him (I'd go by Hammy).

Fran's mom once told me she wanted to name him Vincent, after her Italian mother, Vincenza. 'Cause every boy wants to be named after his grandmother, ahem. Still, Vincent sounded better than Francis to me, but I'm sure after the sheer exhaustion of child-birth, my father-in-law could have named him Quasimodo and she wouldn't have given a shit. (For the record, I think either "Quasi" or "Modo" would have been a lot cooler than "Fran.")

I should apologize right now to everyone who is named Fran-cis, named their kid Francis, or who is a junior or has a junior. (But don't hold your breath.)

Where was I? Oh right, obsessing about my poor, unlucky, no-longer perky left boob.

After I told her about my mammogram, Lola, my **internet friend** (see "old ass"), sent me a *New York Times* op-ed entitled,

"Cancer Survivor or Victim of Over-Diagnosis?"[28] The article was about how women are being treated for breast cancer they don't even have. This over-diagnosis of "early stage pre-cancer" by new digital mammography picks up every teeny, tiny abnormality, leading to treatments like radiation, chemotherapy, or surgery for something that would never have actually made the women sick.

What crappy news. Not only did I need to worry about *having* breast cancer, I also needed to worry about being *over-treated* for breast cancer *I didn't have*. Lola is a fucking peach, isn't she? I wrote her back:

> Thanks a lot, sunshine. How does this even help me? Am I supposed to tell my doctor to shove his chemo up his ass because I'm taking a stand and won't allow my boob to be another victim of modern medicine's overly aggressive diagnosis? Brilliant. Then when I die from breast cancer, I'll be able to say I died fighting the man, so I win.

Lola agreed, and said she'd probably have everything from her neck down removed to be on the safe side.

And fuck you very much, *New York Times*, for making our cancer (?) treatment choices just a little shittier.

As it happened, this was the year the Mayans predicted the world would end on December 21st. I was somewhat ambivalent about it. I figured it'd be pretty ironic if the doctor told me I had three weeks to live, but the earth ended in two. I was also happy to have an excuse for getting out of Christmas parties.

---

[28] I forgot to tell you I met Lola on an internet forum, where we started chatting and found we had a great deal in common. For example, we both love cheese. What are the chances?

When the world didn't end, I was bummed I had to spend *another* six months worrying about breast cancer.[29] Why couldn't the radiologist have said, "All clear. See you in a year"? **#FML** (See "old ass.") On the positive side, I was thinking if my boob never bounced back into its former shape, my next diagnostic mammogram would be a breeze. It'd be like doing a mammogram on an overcooked fettuccini noodle.

Little did I know that there are worse things than having a radiologist tell you to come back in six months. Holy shit! Did I just end this chapter with a cliffhanger?

I did![30]

---

[29] Can you believe the Mayans fucked up their calculations for the end of the world? They seemed so sure. Weren't they supposed to have crazy good math and astronomy skills? Maybe it was a Christmas miracle.

[30] I sure hope pointing it out didn't ruin the effect.

Chapter 3

Getting called into a private room and the unnecessary involvement of a three-armhole gown

SIX MONTHS LATER, I had yet another follow-up mammogram. Most women over forty know the routine. Ta-tas get flattened. You sit and wait, then someone decides they either want more titty-squashing photos of your mammaries, or they send you home.

I got through the first round of breast mashing and headed back to the holding pen to wait for the nurse to tell me (I hoped), "There are no significant changes since your last mammogram. You can get dressed and come back in twelve months."

While waiting, I pretended to read a book on my Kindle, while observing three other women, who were wearing the same, lovely, salmon-colored hospital gown I had on. It was like a cancer-screening edition of "Who Wore It Best?"[31]

Honestly, I had grown enamored of the salmon-colored gowns. The radiology department administrator probably hired an expensive color consultant to do some comprehensive study to determine which color was most calming to patients and would make them feel the least self-conscious about sitting around half-naked next to complete strangers. And to that color expert, I say, *Well done, you!*

I've been in some weird-ass hospital gowns. A couple of times I've come across the kind with *three* armholes, which are *really* difficult to figure out. What fuckin' design genius took what is basically a bathrobe and turned it into something that requires an engineering degree to put on? If you haven't experienced these before, I'm not even shitting you. I took a photo of the instructions in the changing room to show you, but then I decided to draw it, instead, (see drawing below).

Three-Armhole Gown: Instructions

Step 1   Step 2   Step 3

---

[31] If you don't already know, "Who Wore It Best?" refers to a popular segment in gossip columns, magazines, and cable TV shows that love to compare photos of celebrities wearing the same dress, because judging women is one of America's favorite pastimes.

Here's what I looked like after Step 3 (see drawing below).

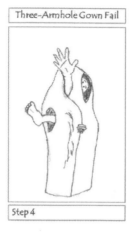

Three-Armhole Gown Fail

Step 4

Granted, I'm no doctor, and maybe doctors see lots of people who are born with the misfortune (or fortune?) of having three arms, but in my limited experience of hospitals—and life—I have never—not once—encountered a person with three arms.[32] And even if there are a few souls out there who are excessively arm-endowed, maybe a better solution would be for the hospital to keep the three-armhole gowns in a special section of the linen closet marked "For Hindu Gods Only," and use the majority of the space for the far more common two-armed patients? Wouldn't that make more sense?

The salmon gowns that I like so much go on like a small jacket and, if you're feeling really saucy, you can show a little cleavage. If

---

[32] A third arm could be a great help, I suppose, depending on where it was. Like, say, if it was on your back, you could fix your wedgies with no one being the wiser. On the other hand, if it was on top of your head, you'd look like you were constantly waving, which could get awkward in crowded bars. You'd also never be able to go to an art auction or be around anyone looking for volunteers.

you're not feeling saucy (and it'd be a *very* odd day at the radiology office if you were), there are plenty of ties at the side that are easy to secure.

Where was I? Oh, right—in the holding pen, waiting to hear if they needed more images. As time progressed, two of the three other women were called. They were taken behind a sort of half-wall that was supposed to provide some privacy, but we could all pretty much hear everything the nurse said, because she was a loud whisperer (you know the type). I don't know what exactly was behind the wall, because I'm not a nosy person,[33] but the first two women were told everything looked fine and they should come back in twelve months.

Shortly thereafter, the last of the other three women was hurried away. She was gone for a few minutes, but she wasn't taken behind the half-wall of privacy, and when she returned, she was fully clothed. She sat down and said, "Geez, now they want to talk to me in a private room. *That* doesn't sound good."

"Oh, no!" I said. We crooked-smiled uneasily at each other, neither of us knowing what else to say, then went back to pretend-reading our books. All I could think was, *Please don't call me into a private room ... please don't call me into a private room.*

My prayers were interrupted when I was called into a private room.

The first thing the nurse said was, "There's nothing to worry about." Pfft ... easy for her to say—it wasn't *her* boob we were looking at.

So I shouted, "ARE YOU FUCKING KIDDING ME? WE'RE IN A PRIVATE ROOM!!!! OF *COURSE* THERE'S SOMETHING TO WORRY ABOUT, YOU INSENSITIVE ASS!

---

[33] Two comfy chairs and a side table with a bunch of breast cancer brochures.

SPIT IT OUT, ALREADY! HOW MUCH TIME DO I HAVE TO LIVE!?!"

Kidding. Luckily, I kept my pie hole shut, because as it turned out, there really wasn't anything to worry about (yet). The nurse said they wanted me to come back for a follow-up mammogram in six months, but that nothing had changed *significantly* since my last images.

So I'm thinking, "What the actual *fuck*, Kaitlyn?![34] Why couldn't you tell me this behind the half-wall of privacy? Why'd you scare me half to death by bringing me into a private room? I hate you and I hope you die on your stair-stepper tonight."

I smiled and thanked her profusely. I thought about slamming the door behind me (right in her stupid WASPY face), since I was angry about having yet another six months of worrying ahead, but instead, I politely held the door for her, and let her exit first. Because I am a fucking lady.

Here comes some personal information that my husband thinks nobody will give a shit about, but which I'll tell you anyway, because it relates to my worrying and how it can manifest physically. Plus, I already went to the trouble of taking a picture, so now I want to use it.[35]

I get tiny anxiety bumps, or blisters, on my hands (see picture below). I suppose I would describe them as little bubbles beneath

---

[34] Yeah ... her name was Kaitlyn, of course. You never meet any young, skinny, irritating, WASP nurses named Gladys or Myrtle. Nope. And if it's not Kaitlyn, it's Brittany or Ashley. Goddammit.

[35] Look at me going the extra mile to take a picture and add it to this book, even though I'm dying of breast cancer. All this, simply to enhance your reading pleasure. That's pretty unselfish of me, if I say so myself. That's how I want to be remembered, Fran: unselfish. Don't forget to add that to my obituary. Thanks in advance, hon.

the skin—almost, but not quite, rash-like—and although they don't itch (much), I have a habit of rubbing my thumb over these tiny lumpa-bumps. Anyway, these "worry blisters" (that's what I call them, though I suspect they're really some sort of flesh-eating bacteria that feeds off of stress) were in full bloom during the week leading up to the slammogram.

Worry blisters. Should I be worried about these?

I asked Google about these blisters, but oddly, Google responded with a lot of irrelevant articles about cold sores and STDs, and then some very frightening sample images. When I did an image search for "worry blisters on fingers," one of the pictures looked suspiciously like a penis. *Because it was a penis!* Immediate **click regret** (see "old ass"). Damn me and my curiosity!

Clearly there was some kind of epic fail going on with Google's image-search algorithm for worry blisters. I hope it's been fixed by now, because nobody who's worrying about worry blisters needs to accidentally see a penis pustule. I had even entered my search phrase in quotation marks, which is supposed to mean, "Only show me pages that contain this exact phrase," and Google *still* thought I might like to see a picture of a penis with a rash on it.

No, Google! Not even close!

The search results also included an advertisement headlined, "Gods [*sic*] Answer to Worry." I saw it and immediately thought, *Oh, I'm definitely not clicking on that.* But then I wondered: What does it say about me as a person that I won't click on that ad? Someone spoke directly to God—presumably, between asking about how to achieve peace in the Middle East and how to end famine—and asked for God's thoughts on worrying, and then went to the trouble of sharing the answer with the **interwebz** (see "old ass"). Shouldn't I be a *little* curious about the message this modern-day prophet has to relay?

Or what if the ad was for God's personal website?! Maybe God had been blogging for years. God might also have a Twitter account, a Facebook page, and maybe a YouTube channel to which I should subscribe. After all, God had to pay Google for the keyword "worry," so God must have thought it important for worriers to find His/Her website straightaway. I should probably read it.

Still, I didn't want to know if God's answer was "Thou shalt not worry," which would be more of a commandment than a helpful answer. What if worrying was a sin? Then I'd worry that my worrying about getting into heaven would ensure that I'd *never* get into heaven (and it would be just my luck that there'd actually be a heaven and they wouldn't let me in). But God probably already thought of this conundrum, so maybe God said, "Thou shalt not worry, for I am a loving God," giving me hope that even though God sees me worrying, and doesn't care for it, God is also an agreeable all-powerful being who will let me into heaven, anyway.

But what if "Thou shalt not worry, for I am a loving God"

meant God was exasperated and was being condescending?[36] As in, "Look, you know I'm a loving God, right? So what are you worrying about? I'm telling you *not* to worry! Quit being so fucking **emo** (see "old ass") or I'll send you directly to the fiery pits of hell for disobeying me." In which case, I'd have plenty of cause for worry.

I decided not to click on the ad. I figured I already had enough things to worry about without adding "Am I going straight to hell for worrying?" to my list. Also because I didn't want to get distracted from finding out whether or not there's a flesh-eating bacteria that starts out as tiny bubbles on fingers and will eventually make your arm fall off. (There is.)

Since I brought up worrying—again—I do have more than a few factors, in addition to my DES exposure, that put me at an increased risk of breast cancer. Quite a few women on both sides of my family have had breast cancer, including my paternal grandmother, two paternal aunts, and one maternal aunt. My mom's sister was getting radiation treatments for her breast cancer around the time I was going in for this mammogram. One of my dad's two sisters had a particularly aggressive form of breast cancer (HER-2 positive) in one of her breasts. She had a mastectomy and chemo—and *two other* types of cancer in her *other* breast (like winning a really shitty lottery—three times!). She went through hell, but is an amazingly brave woman. (Unfortunately, the bravery gene skipped me.)

Also, my dad's mom was an Ashkenazi Jew, which means she may have been a carrier of the BRCA1 gene. I think I read somewhere that one in forty individuals of Ashkenazi Jewish ancestry have this gene. (She had uncles who died in the Holocaust, too, but I don't

---

[36] I'd be condescending, too, if I could shoot people in the ass with a lightning bolt from my finger. If I had that power, I would use it All. The. Time.

think that's transmittable. If it is, my uncles should be *super* careful about getting on trains.)[37] The BRCA1 gene increases the risk of certain types of cancer, including breast cancer. It's the gene Angelina Jolie has.[38]

So, because of my DES exposure, my family history of breast cancer, the fact that I've never had a child, and the fact that I have dense breasts, my risk of getting breast cancer is significantly increased. That's why I feel like I have plenty of reasons to worry (and by "worry," I mean freak out enough to give myself a flesh-eating disease on my fingers).

After I was done trying to find information about my worry blisters, I decided to look on Amazon to see if they sell those salmon-colored hospital gowns. I like to be comfortable while I'm wiggin' out.

Luckily, I started to feel better after about six months. But then I had my follow-up mammogram, which totally ruined it.

---

[37] I was going to add "too soon?" but I know the Holocaust is nothing to joke about. It really isn't. The title of this book should probably be "I'm going straight to hell."

[38] As you may remember, Jolie had a prophylactic double mastectomy, as well as the removal of her fallopian tubes and ovaries. Because she's a badass and doesn't fuck around.

Chapter 4

The advent of the boobarazzi and an excess of information

THE FOLLOWING DECEMBER, ONE year after the Thanksgiving Tit-Smashing Throwdown, I went to my gynecologist, Dr. Phingers (she's from the Philippines) for an annual checkup. This doctor reminds me of the character Edna Mode from Disney's *The Invincibles*—the really short one who designs all the superhero costumes. Dr. Phingers is another one who likes to touch my boobs. Being in my late forties, I should be happy that *anyone* wants to touch my boobs, but I get tired of the routine. I've started referring to these folks as the boobarazzi, because they seem to love looking at, touching, and taking pictures of my boobs. During the exam, Dr. Phingers said she didn't "like the feel" of a lump in my left breast. Ummm, come again? She wasn't happy with *how it felt...*? Seriously? An unhappy boob-touching customer? How often does *that* happen?

A little too often, in my case, and it's enough to give a girl a complex.

So my gynecologist said, as she had a few times in the past, that she would very much like for me to have both my tits smashed, plus an ultrasound on the left one, please. I've noticed she usually gets a concerned look on her face whenever she feels a lump, bless her heart. I remember one time, at the very beginning of a visit, I told her I thought I had a lump. She rushed over and had me lie down so she could feel it. That particular lump turned out to be nothing (I have fibrocystic breasts), but I've always appreciated her sense of urgency.

I scheduled the mammogram and ultrasound for as soon as I could get in, which just happened to be my twenty-fifth wedding anniversary.[39]

So I went for my 123rd (okay, third) six-month follow-up slam-mogram, with a side order of ultrasound. This time, the radiologist on duty saw some "changes" in whatever they had been "watching" for months and months.

Can we take a second here and talk about modern medicine's use of the word "watching"? I don't think it means what they think it means. If I'm asked to "watch" something important—like, say, a toddler—I'm not going to ignore it for six months and then check in to make sure it's all right. It may have gotten itself into all kinds of trouble after only three months. It may even have managed to smear shit all over the bathroom after only five unattended minutes (to my nephew Kyle: You probably don't remember this incident, since you were two, but I'm still impressed with how much you were able to get done in such a brief time). I believe the word the radiologists are actually looking for is "disregard"—as in, "Let's disregard this for *another* six months." (Procrastinating bastards.)

And okay, I realize it's silly of me to expect them to watch my

---

[39] This makes me sound reaaaaallly old, but in my defense, I got married when I was 21. Fran's really old because he was 25 when we married.

breasts *every minute of every day* for signs of cancer. It's not like I wanted them to install a tiny monitor/ultrasound machine in my bra or anything ... that would be ridiculous. (But is it? Note to a certain salesperson at Sears: Just because you've never heard of a "smart bra" doesn't mean it hasn't been invented yet. Luddite).[40] But six months seemed like a long time to ignore something that could be cancer.

Getting back to the wonky mammogram—turns out, the lump my doctor felt was a parasitic twin who'd been living inside me all this time and who now wanted me to rule the galaxy with her. She had architectural plans for a **Death Star** (see "old ass"), capable of blowing up an entire planet, drawn on my spleen. (Turns out, spleens *can* be useful.) She'd been working on it since *Star Wars* came out in 1977 (for a parasitic twin living inside a host's left tit, plotting to rule the universe is pretty much all there is to do). I declined, because can you imagine the cost of the liability insurance alone? Oy.

Too far? Okay, none of that happened, and I hope George Lucas doesn't come after me, but I didn't want the plot to get too predictable. Plus, on a more serious note, there are such things as "dermoid cysts" and "teratoma tumors." I first learned about these when they were mentioned as "possibilities" on a frightening lab report I received about a year later, but that's a topic for volume II, so just go google these phrases. (Warning: Do *not* do an image search. Just don't.) Suddenly, a parasitic twin in my left tit doesn't seem quite so outlandish, does it? It *totally could have happened* ... you know ... in a galaxy far, far away.

All right, here's what *actually* happened after the wonky mammogram. First, I was escorted to another room, where a different

---

[40] By the way, a breast cancer detecting iPhone app would make a fortune. Can you even believe this book? A harrowing cancer tale AND an idea for a money-making invention? You certainly got your money's worth. Tell a friend.

technician performed an ultrasound. When the tech was done, she asked me to wait in the ultrasound room while she went to see if the radiologist needed any further imaging. (I suspect what she was really doing was running down the hall to tell the radiologist that she just saw the largest malignant cancer tumor, *ever*, and figured the doctor would want to see this fuckin' thing before I died and got sent down to the morgue.)

When they both entered *my private room* (yikes!), the radiologist, Dr. Barium, introduced herself. She didn't mention anything about my giant, Guinness record–worthy tumor. I'm sure she didn't want to alarm me. She told me there were a couple of suspicious areas on the mammogram and ultrasound, and she suggested I have a biopsy done by a breast surgeon. Ironically, the whole time she was talking, I was *hoping* she'd say I needed to come back in six months for more "watching." But nope. The boobarazzi had graduated from taking pictures of my breast to wanting *pieces* of it! I should have gotten a restraining order.

After Dr. Barium told me I needed a biopsy, I (rather surprisingly) held my shit together. Still in shock, I suppose. Trying not to sound too shattered, I said, "A biopsy? Well *that* definitely sounds like a reasonable next step. That involves taking a cotton swab of my breast, right? Hehe."

My joke went over like a fart in church. Both the technician and the radiologist looked at me with just the sort of look you'd give to someone who has breast cancer and doesn't know it yet. Their somber faces screamed, "You poor, dumb, naïve idiot."

Dr. Barium explained a little further about what she was seeing on the images. She said some microcalcifications had changed since my last mammogram. Noticing the slight quiver in my bottom lip, the technician sidled closer to a box of Kleenex (no doubt ready to present me with a tissue); the doctor started edging near the phone by the door (no doubt ready to call security for immediate sedation of a patient).

No longer successful at keeping my shit together, I said, "OH MY GAWD, YOU SAW CANCER! GET IT OUT OF ME RIGHT NOW!" in my head.

Out loud, my voice cracked as I said, "Shall I just go and talk to the secretary about scheduling the biopsy, then?"

Dr. Barium suggested I consult with a breast surgeon first. She gave me the card of a woman who specializes in breast cancer, Dr. Cutter. I wasn't exactly certain why I needed any "consulting" before I got the biopsy. I strongly felt the next step should be to page whichever surgeon was on call and start wheeling me toward an operating room straightaway. Last I checked, late-stage metastatic cancer treatment doesn't involve a great deal of talking. Cancer therapy starts with surgery, or radiation, or chemo—not a nice, long chat over a cup of tea (though maybe it should). I made an appointment to "talk" to the surgeon, anyway.

Oh, by the way, guess what I gave Fran for our silver anniversary?

The news that I needed a breast biopsy. (No time to shop.)

ME: They want me to go for a breast biopsy.

FRAN: Oh, shit.

ME: The radiologist did say she was fairly certain what they were seeing were benign calcifications.

FRAN: Oh, well, that's a relief. So the biopsy is just a precaution.

ME: Yeah, but I'm fairly certain that when she used the phrase "fairly certain" it almost certainly meant she wasn't very certain at all, and was only trying to delay my panicked reaction until after she was certain I had left the building.

FRAN: I don't think she'd lie to you.

ME: No, you're right. I'm sure we needn't worry. They probably caught the cancer *kind of* early. Though she did say she wants me to speak to a breast surgeon next, which may mean *she* didn't want to be the one to tell me that I would need a mastectomy and chemotherapy.

I didn't tell Fran what I really thought—that I had stage IV breast cancer that had begun spreading six months prior, while the radiologist "monitored" it—because I wanted Fran to worry just enough so he'd feel the need to pamper me, but not so much that he lost all hope and started wondering how long a reasonable mourning period would be before he could start dating again.

About a week later, I dutifully had my consultation with Dr. Cutter, who—surprise, surprise—*also* wanted to feel my boobs. (Dr. Cutter looked like the kind of person who was in the color guard in her high school marching band and took it *very* seriously.) But actually, I *was* surprised she wanted to touch my boobs, because I thought she was just going to review my mammogram with me. I didn't think it would require any touching. Fortunately, I had shaved that morning, or she would have thought I was a mental case when I refused to raise my arms. (At this point, I should know they all want to feel my boobs and just start disrobing as soon as I sign in at the front desk.)

I was still clinging to a slight hope that the surgeon would tell me she thought the shadows were definitely benign calcifications, but instead, she ended up agreeing with the radiologist that a biopsy was indicated. Wellllll ... every problem looks like a nail (requires a surgical solution) when you're a hammer (surgeon) ... amirite?

DR. CUTTER: The particular lump your gynecologist is feeling is actually a benign cyst. (Pointing to a spot on the ultrasound image.)

ME: So it's not a parasitic twin?

DR. CUTTER: What?

ME: What?

Well, I had to ask, didn't I? At least I learned quickly that she had absolutely *no* sense of humor. She looked at me like I had two heads, both with their hair on fire.

Okay, so a benign cyst. Good to know.

She offered to aspirate the cyst, if it was bothering me. Ho boy ... and so it begins. Surgeons! Always looking for an opportunity to slice into something (or aspirate it ... whatever). Um, no, thank you. I've grown quite attached to Baren (don't you love when twins' names rhyme?). You can keep your oversized, tootling needle out of my breast, and Baren and I will thank you very much for it.

Amazingly, my pie hole remained mostly closed, and I simply said, "No, that's okay. It hasn't been bothering me."

Frankly, why I should want *anything* in my boob aspirated (deflated) is beyond me. If anything, I'd want it *in*spirated ... wouldn't I?

Having dispensed with the good news, Dr. Cutter moved on to the shitty news. Here's how the rest of the conversation proceeded (note: my internal monologue is denoted by the use of asterisks and italics):

DR. CUTTER: (pointing to areas on my mammogram, displayed on a computer screen) These shadows here have the classic appearance of benign calcifications.

ME: Oh, benign, that's good. *That's fuckin' awesome! I like the sound of benign. Benign. Benign. Benign. I even like how the g is silent. I should put a silent g in my name. Karegn.*

DR. CUTTER: But these shadows over here are a bit suspect. They've changed from your last mammogram.

ME: Oh, I see. *Well, hang on. Let's not jump to any conclusions. We all change at one time or another, don't we? It doesn't mean we've turned into cancer. Maybe they've just grown more calcified? Taken some online calcification correspondence classes to improve themselves? Also, I have been drinking a lot of milk with my Lucky Charms lately. Could that have done it? Because I've been meaning to switch to soy.*

(I gave the doctor my most encouraging "Hmmm. You sound very smart. Please go on" look.)

DR. CUTTER: The next step would be to biopsy these areas.

(My encouraging look may have faltered here.)

ME: Well, I suppose that's probably for the best. *Are you out of your fucking mind? Bloody hell that seems unnecessarily invasive. Why go straight to a biopsy? Why not an MRI or an EKG or an ABC? ABC sure sounds like a good place to start.*

(I would have said this last bit out loud, but I wasn't sure what kind of ramifications there might be if the word "nutcase" was added to my medical records.)

She started to describe the biopsy procedure to me, and right then, I tried to stop her by putting my fingers in my ears and singing the "la la la la" song—you know how it goes. (I'm not even kidding this time—I did this out loud, not just in my head. I didn't care if she found it funny or not; I just wanted her to stop.) I made that face you give someone who is over-sharing (which is sort of a cross between a fake smile and a please stop), and I told her, "I don't really need to know the details."

As a matter of general principle, I do *not* want to know the details of medical procedures. I wouldn't watch *Grey's Anatomy* when all my friends at work were talking about it every week, because I don't want to know what happens even in fake hospitals. You know those "The More You Know" public service announcement commercial thingies? Well, I *reaaaally* do not want to know. They say, "The more you know," as if it's a good thing, and it's *not*, people; it's really not. Especially when it comes to medical shit.[41] If I need to have a test done, I don't want you to tell me what you are doing or even why you are doing it—just point me at the machine and let me know when it's over.

At my refusal to hear the details, Dr. Cutter's face somehow grew *even more serious*. (Color me surprised—I didn't think she could get *even more* serious.) It may be because she didn't like being interrupted. It wouldn't have surprised me to learn she had her

---

[41] If you think I'm crazy, try asking your doctor if there are any complications that could arise during your upcoming "routine" surgery. I guarantee you'll regret asking that question. I once asked a surgeon about possible complications from neck surgery, to "fix" my herniated disc. He said, "Well, of course, there's always a slight risk of death whenever you go under general anesthesia." So I said, "Sure, but there are things worse than death." He replied, "Okay, there's a small chance of paralysis." I almost knocked him over as I ran out the door.

speech memorized, and when interrupted, she had to start again from the beginning. Instead, slightly exasperated, she said, "But I need to tell you what to expect."

I must have looked a lot like a deer caught in headlights, struck by a car, and then hauled off to a surgeon's office, where the deer was reluctantly forced to listen to the doctor explain all the details of its upcoming antler-ectomy (see drawing below).

Oh deer.

Dr. Cutter ignored my expression, started over undaunted, and told me the procedure is called a "stereotactic core needle biopsy" (which I now know is like boob acupuncture—only it's acupuncture with a really huge needle; it involves few, if any, kindly old Chinese people; it will do absolutely nothing to balance my chi; and it has the exact opposite effect of reducing pain). Oh, and by the way, they are using the word "needle" here very loosely. I'd say it's closer to one of those drills they use to get ice core samples in Antarctica. They have to make an incision in your skin with a scalpel before they can insert it into your breast, so yeah, "needle" my ass.

Dr. Cutter said the procedure would require me to lie facedown on a table. My breast would drop through a hole, similar to a cow being trapped in a squeeze chute before getting branded, or so I gathered. I would have thought she was kidding, but I knew she had no sense of humor (or didn't share my sense of humor—same thing), so I didn't make the "glory hole without the happy ending" joke that popped into my head. If you don't know what a glory hole is, I assure you that you don't want to know, because, again, the more you know is never a good thing![42]

Still don't believe me? Try googling a study done by the University of Arizona that examined bacteria on shopping cart handles, where they found that 72% of the shopping carts had "a marker for fecal bacteria." That's right, they found evidence of *shit* on shopping cart handles. Now go ahead and try to tell me your life just got better for knowing that. Also, it sounds like a whole lot of people are pushing their shopping carts wrong.

Though I successfully avoided mentioning glory holes, I did snort a little, and I said something along the lines of "Seriously?" The deadpan look on her face told me she was very serious. She handed me a brochure with a picture of a woman lying on a table with her boob dangling through a hole. I drew it for you (see drawing below).

---

[42] And for the love of all that is holy, stay away from the online **Urban Dictionary**! (See "old ass.")

Boobarazzi: Like wildebeest to a watering hole, they gather round to witness a core needle biopsy.

The description of the procedure grew steadily worse. On the other side of the ~~glory~~ boobie-hole, there's some x-ray–type apparatus (metal clamp) that performs a mammogram *during* the biopsy.

I was like … "Um, wait … so the whole time you're doing this, you're going to be squeezing the shit out of my tit?"

The surgeon implied that I was wrong (I wasn't) and quickly corrected me. *Compressing*, she said. They would be *compressing* my breast.

So, in summary, she was going to compress the shit out of my boob while sticking a big, honking needle into it and poking around for about forty-five minutes (I asked), so she could then violently (my word, not hers) amputate (biopsy) a huge chunk of it (I'm paraphrasing). And here comes the worst part: I'd be wide awake the whole time! (Barbaric!) I wanted to ask her why she didn't just take the entire boob, since modern medicine seemed to love it so much, but I was afraid she might say okay.

So we scheduled the biopsy for early January. Need I say it? I was incredibly anxious. It was a couple of weeks away, and what if I didn't live that long? What if my cancer was already spreading, and we missed the window for doing a double mastectomy followed by radiation, chemotherapy, and an all red beet diet, which would surely have stopped the cancer's progression to my brain and saved my life?!

I felt a headache coming on.

There was sooo much to worry about—so many things that could go wrong. Since worrying is like my religion, here's how I'd pray, if I were the praying type: "Dear Universe, during my biopsy, please don't let me get necrotizing fasciitis that my doctor picked up while volunteering in Africa for Doctors Without Borders ... and please don't let me get the shits ... especially not the shits ... because having a flesh-eating disease would suck, sure, but having the runs on the glory-hole table in front of the surgeon and nurses would be mortifying. Lord, hear my prayer."

Unfortunately, I'm not the praying type. I'm more of a non-practicing optimist.

And it's true that Dr. Cutter worked for Doctors Without Borders. It said so in her brochure. A more suspicious person than I *cough*Lola*cough* might assume that the doctor put that in there because it sounds a lot better than saying, "She spends three months out of every year golfing in Acapulco."

But that's ridiculous. Who spends three months golfing in Acapulco? One or two, sure, but not three. No, once I carefully weighed all the evidence (like Dr. Cutter's love of describing surgical procedures in great detail, her collection of brochures with illustrations of boob biopsy devices, and her lack of humor), the answer was staring me right in the face: She's a sadistic international serial killer.[43] It's always the severely repressed ones who let their freak flags fly on vacation, and they didn't come any more uptight than Dr. Cutter.

I know what you're thinking. If Sherlock Holmes had a baby with "the smart one" from *Charlie's Angels* (i.e., the one least likely to be scantily clad), that kid wouldn't have solved this case as quickly as I just did. I'm certain that Dr. Cutter travels to places like Mozambique to perform gruesome experiments on unsuspecting locals because people there lack access to medical malpractice attorneys, and it's probably easy to lure them into a van with some clean bottled water. But the absolute worst part of all this is that I won't be able to reach her when my breast inevitably falls off after my surgery, because she'll be on another Doctors Without Borders working vacation/killing spree!

After the far too informative consultation with the breast surgeon, I figured I needed a prescription for Xanax, so I'd have it for the day of the biopsy (and every goddamned minute of every goddamned day leading up to it). I went to my general practitioner's office the next morning. It's a group practice with several doctors, and I abhor all of them, with the exception of one female doctor, who I really like, Dr. Fein. (She's not actually Jewish, but that's fine.)[44] She listened very patiently, without even rolling her eyes. She handed me a box of tissues while I cried and told her how worried I was about the upcoming biopsy, until I finally got to the point, which was: Tranquilize me now, please.

I thought Xanax would help me relax a bit more and worry a

---

[43] Remember that asshole dentist who killed Cecil the Lion? I bet that douche nozzle told his patients he was volunteering for Dentists Without Borders every time he went on a big game hunt.

[44] I don't know why I find this funny, but I do.

bit less; I was having a hard time getting to (and remaining) asleep. But later, Lola told me how terribly addicting Xanax can be. She said some people have gotten addicted to it within a couple of weeks—so then I started worrying about getting addicted to Xanax. It was an anxiety catch-22 clusterfuck.

Strangely (or maybe the right word here would be naturally), another thing that had me terribly worried about the core needle biopsy came from what the literature said about pain during and after the procedure. While most women feel very minor discomfort from the tissue removal (#FalseAdvertising),[45] they can experience "some pain" in the neck and back afterward from lying facedown with their head turned to one side for the duration of the procedure. Because I have a herniated disc in my neck, I am terrified it might become "angry" again and impinge on the nerve. That's the kind of pain that could make a person want to tap out on life. Like, if suicide bombers suffered from sciatica, I can totally understand why they'd push the button. I get it. I just wish they'd do it in private. Wait. What? *(That took a dark turn.)*

So, as frightening as the prospect of having breast cancer was, I was even more worried about my neck. The very last thing I needed was to have surgery on my neck. Call me crazy, but I've got a serious phobia of quadriplegia. Dying slowly from cancer? Yes, that would totally suck. But being unable to move or scratch an itch? That would literally (and I do mean literally) send me to the loony farm. It's my worst nightmare, and I've watched *The Texas Chainsaw Massacre*—both the original *and* the remake.

It's true that my mind tends to go right to the worst-case scenario (like quadriplegia resulting from neck surgery needed after a breast biopsy), and maybe I *do* tend to wallow in my misery before

---

[45] Newsflash: "Breast Biopsy Causes Little Discomfort, Says Big Fat Liar."

I've even gotten to anything miserable, but on the plus side, I'm *always* prepared for a shitstorm.

On the bright side, other than disfigurement, an untimely death from an exotic staph infection, and quadriplegia, I had no worries at all about the upcoming biopsy.

Chapter 5

DES and deja boo—a cancer-scare tale told through bad and/or misunderstood cliches

IN THIS CHAPTER, MY gynecologist throws some **shade** at my cervix (see "old ass"), then gets mad when I seek a second opinion, 'cause that bitch be **cray** (see "old ass").

Just for fun, I thought I'd turn this chapter into a drinking game, using malapropisms and/or misunderstood cliches. If you want to play along, take a drink every time I bastardize a cliche. You should definitely try this at home. What's the worst that can happen? You get drunk, attempt some impossible feat, fail miserably (because it was impossible, duh), your "friend" posts it on YouTube, it goes viral, and everybody wins.[46]

---

[46] If you do post a video, please use the hashtag #PointlessBoob. Let's break the internet! Also, Fran reminded me, for legal purposes, I should maybe be clear that when I say, "You should definitely try this at home," I mean don't.

Before we begin, I'd like to mention that I honestly wrote this chapter before I read Mamrie Hart's Book, "You Deserve a Drink," which has a built-in drinking game throughout (if you like to laugh, go read it). So I'm not plagiarizing, but I *did* get my inspiration from her YouTube channel (I may not know what plagiarism actually means). My writing isn't derivative, either. I'm simply imitating her work. It's called *flattery*.

After I read Mamrie's book, I thought about getting rid of my drinking game, but by that time I'd had a few shots, and thought *screw that*. I participated in college drinking games when Mamrie was still in a high chair, eating pureed peas off a tiny, "flying" spoon.[47] So I decided to leave it in. Maybe someone who has read both books will be outraged and notify Mamrie. Then she'll read my book and love it so much that she'll agree to do the TV miniseries, and we'll become besties on the set. We'll share a huge trailer with two en-suite bathrooms and demand that our dogs get artesian spring water, imported from Norway. (A fully stocked bar goes without saying, but we're fine with mason jars, 'cause we're not fuckin' divas, y'all.)[48] Or her publisher will sue me, and I'll issue a press release that says, "Big Publisher Sues Small Independent Author in a Douche Move." Then even more people will buy my book, because publicity, right?

After another shot, I was like, "Pffft ... fuck you, large publishing house, I will not cease and desist."

Then I laughed at the publisher for daring to take me on in

---

[47] We always fall for the "open up the hangar" trick when someone makes airplane noises. It's like some kind of weird magic. I should try it on Fran next time he doesn't want to eat my eggplant parmesan.

[48] Don't think for a minute that I won't pick up her Southern accent when we start drinking together, because I will. I will pick it up faster than a one-legged man in an ass-kicking competition.

court. Bah, I've been watching *Law & Order* for years. I'll object to anything and everything that might hurt my case. (They don't stand a chance.) After another shot, I couldn't come up with a single downside.[49]

So let's begin. I knew I shouldn't *jump to any delusions* that my upcoming biopsy would result in a malignancy. (Drink! And by the way, crappy/misunderstood cliches or malapropisms will be *in bold and italics*, so you can't miss 'em.)[50] But I'd been there, done that (if "that" means I had the shit scared out of me by some pre-cancerous cells on my cervix years before), because opportunity only knocks once, unless opportunity happens to be cancer that's trying to end you. The first gynecologist I ever went to (let's call her Dr. Howdareyoo), looked in my hoo hoo and said "Oh," using exactly the tone of voice you don't want to hear from someone who is looking in your hoo hoo. Dr. Howdareyoo looked exactly like Dame Edna, if Dame Edna looked even more like a cartoonish exaggeration of an old lady and wasn't able to keep her lipstick inside the lines.

Then she told me that my cervix "looked unusual." **Dafuq** (see "old ass")? She took one gander, and "unusual" was the first word that popped out of her mouth?

She continued to examine my vajay jay like it might have been some type of rare magical creature from a Harry Potter book. Great. Just what I needed. More body parts to be self-conscious about.

---

[49] Pro tip: One fun side effect of playing drinking games is that you'll find all your ideas are brilliant, and you become a fearless idiot.

[50] Except, once you're drunk, all of this text might look like it's in bold and italics, in which case, you win.

Now I was getting judged for how my cervix looked. Geez. Apparently, *beauty is in the eye of the one who beholdin' the speculum.*[51]

Dr. Howdareyoo was the doctor who first told me about DES. She explained that my deformed cervix was likely the result of being exposed to the drug in utero. This news was about **as welcome as a skunk's turd in a punchbowl at a lawn party.**[52] I turned whiter than Johnny Winter's ghost, but she wasn't lyin'. DES does make your cervix look weird. Thanks, DES. You dick.

Dr. Howdareyoo drew a picture of a normal, "healthy cervix," and then she drew mine (see drawing below).

My cervix and I have a lot in common.

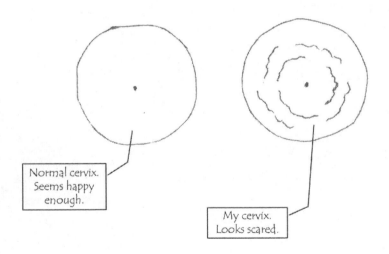

Normal cervix. Seems happy enough.

My cervix. Looks scared.

---

[51] I'm not going to keep telling you when to drink. We're going to use the honor system from now on. But if I were going to tell you, that would have been one more. Just sayin'.

[52] I just combined "turd in a punchbowl" and "skunk at a lawn party" into one stupid cliche. We need to pace ourselves if we want ~~to pretend~~ to drink responsibly.

As I mentioned earlier, DES (diethylstilbestrol) is a synthetic estrogen that was prescribed to pregnant women to prevent miscarriages. It was introduced around 1940. Of course, later, around 1960, doctors and pharmaceutical companies started to give thalidomide to pregnant women for morning sickness, and we all know how shitty that turned out.[53]

In 1953, a study found that DES did *not* prevent miscarriages (that's right, nineteen *fifty fuckin' three*!). So, by the late 1960s, it should have been well known that DES didn't work, but a few doctors, including my mom's, were lazy assholes, and kept prescribing it, anyway. I was born in 1967, and Dr. Howdareyoo was very surprised that I had been exposed to DES.

Ya wanna know what's wrong with our health care system? Doctors prescribing drugs that do nothing, or that have shitty side effects, like making cervixes look weird. Science seems to think there's no lady problem that can't be fixed by throwing a little fake estrogen at it, as though an **ounce of prevention is worth a pound of misshapen cervixes.**

In the sixties, doctors started identifying clusters of girls—as young as seven—who had developed a rare vaginal cancer due to DES exposure, and the FDA reticently issued a letter (an official Drug Bulletin) in 1971, "suggesting" doctors stop giving it to pregnant women (I guess the FDA doesn't like to sound too bossy). I'd been born after these young girls got vaginal cancer, yet my mom's doctor and others were either unconvinced or remained ignorant of the drug's dangerous side effects. Or maybe they wanted 'Merica to

---

[53] *They prescribed it for fucking morning sickness!* I guess water and crackers hadn't been invented yet. (My editor noted that some women get such severe morning sickness that they end up in the hospital on IVs, and that reading this footnote may cause them to hunt me down. Please don't hunt me down.)

lead the world again in birth defects (or childhood vaginal cancer). I'm about as dumb as a bag of blondes, and even I could have told you it might not be a good idea to give drugs to a pregnant woman.

So Dr. Howdareyoo said I should get Pap smears weekly (or maybe she said every six months). She said I ~~would probably die from~~ was at a higher risk for certain types of cancers, including cervical, breast, ovarian, and vaginal cancer. Yeah, and holy what the fuck, she actually said cancer of the vagina. Call me an idiot, but even though I'd heard of breast and cervical cancers, I'd never heard of vajayjay cancer. Eeeeeek! Vaginal cancer has seriously got to be the scariest-sounding cancer in the world. It was just like FDR once so famously put it: The only thing we have to fear is fear of rogue cancers of the lady-parts.

I was more than a little shocked by the news, and it definitely scared the shit out of me. When I left the doctor's office, I called my mom and asked her if she knew anything about DES and if she had taken it when she was pregnant with me? Mom immediately started to cry. Then I started to cry. Then we both agreed that exposure to DES had greatly increased our risk of crying. It also increased my risk of wishing ill on her smug, self-righteous doctor (I had little doubt he was smug and self-righteous), who pushed fake estrogen on my mom back in the late sixties. Especially considering she had already had a successful pregnancy and a healthy baby boy (my older brother). Dafuq, doc?

Here's a fun fact: My mom's doctor was later murdered (allegedly) by his second wife. I became so obsessed with this story that I temporarily forgot about the possibility that I had cervical cancer. Awesome, right? (I'm always looking for the *silver linings playbook*.) My mom started seeing this arrogant prick of a doctor (a distinguished OB/GYN in Philadelphia, named Dr. Fried) after she'd had at least one miscarriage. One of the engineers my dad worked with said Dr. Fried was "The Best" (never trust a *mathemusician*).[54] He specialized in infertility (along with giving women and girls cancer, apparently). So I suppose if my parents were looking for "The Best," and if "The Best" meant an asshole who they paid way too much to give their child a transplacental carcinogen, and who was later killed (allegedly) by his second wife ... then they hit the jackpot.

Dr. Fried really was killed by his wife (allegedly). My mom *heard it through the grapefruit.* We may never know why his wife did it (allegedly), but I bet it's because he gave her vajayjay cancer. When someone gives you cancer of the vagina, it puts you in a pretty crappy mood. I was hoping he came home from work one day and said, "Hey, honey, what's for dinner?"

And his wife said, "I didn't make dinner, because you gave me cancer, asshole. Eat this." Then shot him in the face.

He may not have gotten his dinner that night, but he'd have certainly gotten his *just desserts.* Did you see what I did there? No? Well, you would have, and you'd have found it very amusing, if you'd been drinking along with me.

I'm not judging Mrs. Fried. I'm sure her husband deserved it, and I'm kinda glad she killed him (allegedly). *Live by the sword, die by being gored,* I always say.[55]

I read as many articles about the doctor's death as I could find on the Google machine (because googling is a great way to avoid being productive). The doctor's wife (who was twenty years younger

---

[54] I realize that wasn't a cliche, but it *was* a malapropism, so drink 'em if you got 'em.

[55] I almost never say that, but it was time for another cliche.

than her husband) had not one, but *three* trials.[56] In the first trial, a convict testified that Mrs. Fried had tried to hire him to kill her husband, but he declined, presumably because even though he became a convict, he was not a killer. He went on to testify that Mrs. Fried later told him she'd killed her husband herself, with a pillow (allegedly).

Getting pillowed to death doesn't sound too bad.[57] Is hitting someone with a pillow even a crime? (Is assault with a deadly comforter a thing, too?) Do you get extra jail time if you commit a robbery while armed with a throw? If you poked someone in the chest or gave them a wedgie while robbing them, sure, but crimes committed with a pillow shouldn't be treated with anything more than *a slap on the wheesht*[58] and maybe an hour of community service, **imho** (see "old ass").

I also read that the doctor had a long-time drug and alcohol problem. I say if he was too sloshed to notice he was being smothered with a pillow, whose fault was it, really?[59] If I had to choose between

---

[56] The italics used here were just to emphasize the number of trials, and not to point out a cliche, but at this point, who gives a shit? Have another drink.

[57] Unless you get bludgeoned with a memory foam pillow. Those things could crack a few skulls.

[58] Wheesht is a Scottish word used like this: "Haud your wheesht." It means shut your mouth, or bite your tongue. That doctor deserved a slap on the wheesht, at the very least. (Although I think the word wheesht can also be used as an exclamation on its own, as in "hush," so maybe I should have said "a slap on his wheesht maker?" The Scottish language is so confusing.)

[59] Note: The first step to admitting you're a drunk is acknowledging you can't even fend off someone who's coming after you with a pillow. Step two would be reconsidering your choices if you're playing a drinking game in a book.

death by vaginal cancer and death by pillow, I'd choose pillow all day, every day. Look up the doc and his wife, if you're interested/don't believe me. Their real names were Dr. Paul Fried and Catherine Fried (I bet Fried means "quack who drugs pregnant women" in German). In Catherine's first two trials, she was found guilty, but in her third trial (fourteen years after the doctor's death), she was acquitted. Good on her, I say. And I'm glad she didn't have a fourth trial, because I think after fourteen years, you should *let sleeping docs die.*[60]

I don't know why I have this morbid fascination with Dr. Fried's (alleged) murder, other than that cancer scares make me think about dark things. I felt really bad for my mom. She was guilt-ridden, though she needn't have been. It wasn't her fault. (She had an alibi for the whole pillow/murder thing.)

Even my dad thought Dr. Fried was an asshole, and he rarely calls anyone an asshole, unless they're a mass murderer or Rush Limbaugh. Dad said Dr. Fried had a terrible bedside manner.

For example, after my brother's birth, as the doctor was sewing up my mom "down there," my dad saw her flinch, in obvious pain. Dad asked the doctor to give her a local anesthetic before continuing, but Dr. Fried told him, "No need, this doesn't hurt."

Yep, lied straight to my dad's face. With my mom right there. Dad apparently asked a few too many prickly questions, because he wasn't allowed in the room when I was being born. The doctor didn't want to be second-guessed is my guess. Arrogant jackass.

If Dr. Fried hadn't already been dead, I might have tried to track him down and whack him myself (did I mention I'm one quarter eye-talian? We know how to hide a body)—that's how scared and

---

[60] Sorry. That one was really bad. J/K, I'm not really sorry. #SorryNot-Sorry

mad I was about the whole DES thing. Well, okay, I wouldn't have killed him, but I would definitely have given him a sharp poke in the chest with a very stiff pointer finger, and I'd also have given him the Italian high salute (see drawing below—the high salute is on the right) for good measure.

Italian Sign Language: Go Fuck Yourself

When you mean it   When you really mean it

It took months after learning about my DES exposure before my fears of getting cancer eased. But unfortunately (and inevitably, I suppose), things *took a turn for the liverwurst, the bottom wheel fell off, the curtain flew, the other foot fell, all hell broke free,* AND *the shit hit the admirer.* (If there's a Pulitzer Prize for having the most muddled cliches in a sentence, I just won.) I received some "abnormal results" from a routine Pap smear.

The back of my head shitsploded. I freaked out more than a 1950s Catholic girl with a positive pregnancy test. I was *scareder than a long-tailed cat in a room full of super judgmental normal-tailed cats.*

Dr. Howdareyoo told me she needed to perform a colposcopy, using an intrusive magnification device, called a colposcope. The goal was to locate any suspicious areas on my cervix, rip them out, and send them to a lab.[61] The colposcopy would be done in a place like the Lowell Observatory in Flagstaff, AZ (or the doctor's office in West Chester). I drew a picture of the colposcope (see drawing below).[62]

I do not like your colposcope.
I do not like it, nope, nope, nope.

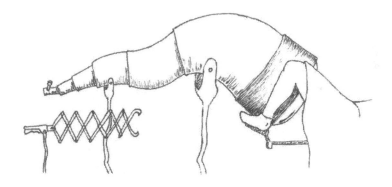

Dr. Howdareyoo told me it wasn't going to hurt, but a colposcopy hurts way worse than being beaten with a pillow. To begin with, it's incredibly uncomfortable to lie with a speculum holding your vagina open for like 40 minutes. Also, when the doctor rips off

---

[61] I later learned these procedures were called punch biopsies. I think the snipping device should come in different shapes, like hearts and stars, to give women a choice of cervical scarring. (It's possible that I'm a little too concerned about the appearance of my cervix now.)

[62] Fran thought my drawing looked Dr. Seuss-ish. My apologies to Theodor Geisel (R.I.P.), who is one of my favorite authors/artists.

a piece of your cervix, there's a very sharp pain. And my doctor fucking well knew it would hurt, because right before she'd take a tissue sample, she'd ask me to hold still, and she had a nurse hold my hand. Both of which indicated that my chances of holding still were about to go way down.

There were actually three people in the room. Two doctors (who happened to be husband and wife) and a nurse. Why they didn't also invite the secretary to join in remains a mystery. Fuckin' bunch of Fibbing McLiarsons. Just before each snip, I'd hear, "Now, this shouldn't hurt, Mrs. McCool." Promises, promises.

The oft-told lie, "This won't hurt a bit" has been proffered to unsuspecting patients since the very first quacks decided bloodletting was a great method of treating sick people. As if sick people didn't already have enough problems. (Granted, having your arm sliced open would certainly take your mind off your stomachache.) I bet these "doctors" were the same guys who thought drilling holes in the heads of the mentally ill was a fantastic way to cure psychiatric disorders.[63] Since then, it's been nothing but **the same old song and lance.** I remember once, when I was kid, I had really huge, poison ivy blisters between my fingers. The doctor decided he needed to cut off the blisters, since pricking them with sterile needles and trying to drain them hadn't worked, and they kept filling up again with a clear-ish liquid and getting even larger. (I know! Ew ew ew!) The doctor told my mom it wouldn't hurt, because it was all dead skin. Dead skin, my ass! Never trust a doctor. Though, in the doctor's defense, if he *had* told me it was going to hurt, it would have taken ten times as long, and there is no insurance billing code for "additional

---

[63] And if you really need evidence of how shitty the medical profession can be, the neurologist who invented the lobotomy won the Nobel Prize for Medicine in 1949. (The Swedish Academy really got snookered *that* year.)

time needed to subdue a patient."

During my colposcopy, Dr. Howdareyoo took between six and a thousand chunks of my cervix to be sent to a lab. And okay, whatever, maybe I *am* a lily-livered coward, but it was a particularly petrifying procedure.[64] Afterward, they told me to take some Tylenol every four hours (stingy with the goddamned heroin, these people), so it couldn't have been that horribly painful, but as I recall, *it fucking well was that horribly painful.*

After about a week, I got the lab results, which showed a bunch of bastardous[65] cells (or maybe they called it severe dysplasia?). I forget the medical term now.[66] But they found some rogue cells in the biopsied tissue, which were considered "pre-cancerous." Not wanting to leave these cells to become cancer, and also to be sure they weren't accompanied by any "postcancerous" cells (they maybe just call those cancer), Dr. Howdareyoo wanted to do a larger biopsy, called a "cervical conization," also known as a "cervical mutilation" (but only by me).

For the conization, the doctor was going to use a scalpel (Lawd Geesus) to remove a cone-shaped section from my cervix. If you don't already know, a conization is to cervixes what a lumpectomy is to breasts.

After speaking with a few family members and friends, I was

---

[64] That's right. I used a little alliteration there, because I am poetic as fuck.

[65] Bastardous is a new word I thought I had coined, but my editor pointed out, it's already in the Urban Dictionary. Even if I can't trademark it, I love this word. It's a real time saver. Instead of having to say "That treacherous bastard of a waiter forgot to give me my salad dressing on the side," you can just call him a bastardous waiter. Brilliant.

[66] Playing this drinking game while trying to write was not my brightest idea.

urged to get a second opinion, and to maybe look into having a gynecological oncologist perform the surgery. That seemed reasonable. And getting a second opinion happens all the time.

But when I told Dr. Howdareyoo I wanted a second opinion, she was like, "How dare you!"

She gave me the stink eye when I went to the office to pick up a copy of my lab report.[67] I don't know if *all* doctors get huffy when you tell them you want a second opinion, but Dr. Howdareyoo sure did.

This pissed me off. When I later called her office to ask them to forward my medical records to my new gynecologist (I wasn't ever going back to Dr. Howdareyoo after this bullshit), the secretary, who was bastardous, seemed to be trying to make my life difficult, and asked me to spell my name.

So I said, "K as in Kill. A as in angry. R as in raging. E as in emotional. N as in nuclear ...." (Not tryin' to brag, but being passive-aggressive is one of my talents. As is being aggressive-aggressive.)

I ended up going to a surgical specialist/gynecologic oncologist in New Jersey, who came highly recommended as an expert in treating cervical cancer. His name was Dr. Pompousass (probably from the Greek island of Jerkopolous or Dickheadapelego). The moment I met him, I thought, "What a nauseatingly pompous asshole you are."

I noticed he had pictures of himself with his Ferrari on every wall of his office. (Over-compensate much?)[68] So my first impression

---

[67] I initially wrote, "She gave me the hairy eyeball," because I think it sounds funnier, but Fran said it didn't. So I took an unofficial poll of a few friends and Fran was right. But don't tell him.

[68] He's lucky my dad was with me that day or I would have said, "Sorry about your penis," on my way out.

turned out to be 100% correct. He was, without a doubt, an extraordinarily patronizing man. I bet all the arrogant, stuck-up prick doctors call *him* an arrogant stuck-up prick behind his back.

With the doctor's approval, I brought my dad with me to New Jersey, because I wanted someone else to hear what the surgeon had to say (and because I need adult supervision). I get so worried at doctors' visits that I sometimes have trouble with comprehension. There have been many a time I've returned home from a doctor's appointment only to have a conversation with Fran that goes something like this:

FRAN: How did it go?

ME: He told me I'm about to die!

FRAN: Are you sure? The doctor said you're going to die?

ME: He may have said there's nothing wrong and to come back in 12 months, I don't recall his exact words.

So this time, to avoid any confusion on Fran's part, I wanted a second set of ears for the visit, and since I didn't want Fran to have to take *another* day off work (he was already planning to take a day off when I had my surgery), I had Dad drive me for the first visit. (Plus, I may have lost a little credibility with Fran when I told him a colposcopy is *exactly* the same as female genital mutilation. He claims it's not. *Tomayto, tom-ah-to.*)

After Dr. Pompousass did the examination, we met in his office. Through body language, he conveyed that he didn't understand why we needed a "meeting." He was incredibly impatient about answering questions, as if he was Donald Trump and I was Megyn Kelly at the Republican primary debate in the summer of 2015. The chorus to Jimmy Buffet's "The Asshole Song" was playing on a loop in my head.

Dr. Pompousass plopped down in his chair and said, "So, you definitely need a cervical conization. You had questions?"

I felt like I'd been called into the principal's office to explain myself. Honest to God, if it was a TV drama and this guy was cast as a self-important, pretentious knob of a doctor, the critics would have slammed his performance for being too over-the-top.

I asked Dr. Pompousass to explain the colposcopy results to me and my dad. I had a notepad and pencil ready. He explained. Briefly. He also showed us a picture of a "healthy" cervix, which kind of looks like the top of a pink balloon with a depressed hole in the center. Then he showed us a picture of *my* cervix.[69] Can you believe he took a picture of my cervix, which, incidentally, looks like that mask from the movie "Scream" (see drawing below).

It'll be fine, they said.
This won't hurt a bit, they said.

---

[69] By the way, he had an entire three-ring binder full of photos of cervixes. What kind of sick, bastardous … ? I can't even.

I *hate* having my picture taken! I'd have been horrified if Fran had seen it. (Do these furrows on my cervix make me look freakish?) It looked like a crime-scene photo. The only thing missing was some police tape around my vagina. It was hideous, especially compared to a healthy cervix. It positively ***paled in compactness.*** He might as well have compared a picture of Jennifer Aniston in a bikini to one of Honey Boo Boo's mom in a muumuu and shower cap. If my cervix were a person, it could have starred in the movie *Freaks.* ("Gooble gobble one of us," fer sher.)

I hope that insensitive bastard has destroyed my photo by now. I don't like anyone having *any* photos of me, and the thought that, somewhere on this planet, there exists a notebook with an image of a repulsive cervix with my name underneath it makes me queasy. If I ever become President, and the supreme leader of Iran threatens to leak that photo to the press unless I give him nuclear weapons, I'd have to consider it.[70]

Anyway, after seeing the glossy, full-color image of my cervix, I was even more certain I wanted the whole mutant thing destroyed immediately. My cervix was like a cancer bomb waiting to explode in the back of my vageen. Dr. Pompousass said he would remove a small portion (the conization process Dr. Howdareyoo had discussed), but he would be doing a "laser conization" instead of using a "cold knife."

At first I thought he said a lightsaber conization, and I was kind of impressed. (Yes. I do love *Star Wars* a little too much.)

I said, "Why not use an X-Acto knife?" (*I like how it implies precision, right in its name.*)

---

[70] However, I'd never sell them anti-tank and anti-aircraft missiles during an arms embargo in exchange for hostages to fund Contra rebels in direct violation of U.S. law, because I'm not an asshole.

Dr. Pompousass ignored me and went on to say the laser conization was a more conservative procedure than a cold knife cone biopsy. He said it would remove less tissue, which would increase my chances of getting pregnant and carrying a child to term later.[71] *Soooo, you're going to potentially leave behind some cancer cells that could kill me, on the off chance that I'll want to have a kid later? Yeah, that sounds reasonable—dude, are you fucking kidding me?*[72]

I was 26 at the time, had been married for 5 years, and *knew* I didn't want to have any kids. I never wanted to have kids. Even as a kid, I didn't like kids. I played with dolls a handful of times because it was the only game the little girl across the street ever wanted to play, and my mom strongly encouraged it, but my heart was never in it. I preferred playing cops and robbers, even though every time I "shot" one of my brothers, they'd say I missed. (I didn't.)

I emphatically denied that I'd ever want kids, but Dr. Pompousass cut me off. "Well, you're only in your twenties, and you don't know what you'll want later."[73]

Um, Houston, we're about to have a major problem. Get an engineer on the line who can tell me how to cobble together a pillow-weapon capable of killing this asshole using only upholstery found in a doctor's office.

I tried to reiterate that I was concerned about my high risk for cervical cancer, given my DES exposure, and I asked him *not* to be conservative with the treatment or with how much of my cervix he removed. He could remove **the hole enchilada** as far as I was con-

---

[71] Wait … having the procedure done with a scalpel would mean I'd have trouble getting pregnant? That. I want that.

[72] I thought the back of my head was going to explode.

[73] This is when the back of my head exploded.

cerned. (And yes, that was a euphemism for my cervix.) We continued to argue about it. Or rather, one of us continued to argue about it. The other one sat behind his desk and rolled his eyes. He pooh-poohed all of my concerns, told me I was still young, and had there not been a large desk between us, I'm certain he would have patted me on the head and called me "little lady."

This absolutely infuriated me, but he wouldn't listen. Well, he did have a penis, after all, so he must know better than me. (Asshole.) My dad was no help. He thinks anything a doctor says is divinely inspired.

I should write Dr. Pompousass a letter now, twenty years later, letting him know how incredibly wrong it was not to allow an adult woman to make her own decisions about her medical treatment—especially when it comes to the potential for cervical cancer. Honestly, how dare he tell *any* woman he's going with a more conservative approach, because *he* decided she'll probably want kids later! (Really, ~~dick~~ doc?)

But he's such a patronizing turd, he'd probably write back and say, "Listen toots, since you don't have cancer yet, I obviously removed exactly the right amount from your cervix, you moron."

Then I'd be pissed that he called me a moron, and I suck at pillow murders, so I'd probably just end up complaining to Fran and sulking about it for weeks.

Well, we'll see **who gets the last laugh** when I actually *get* cervical cancer, ha!

Errr ... wait...

Anyway, Dr. Pompousass went on to tell me he would be doing the surgery in his office, and that I'd be awake for the entire procedure. He said he'd use a local anesthetic, so there "wouldn't be any pain."

Pfft ... It's like he *wanted* to get punched in the dick. So I said,

"Oh geez, I totally missed the joke. I thought you just said I would be awake while you use a laser on my cervix. Ha! Who has two thumbs and is a complete idiot? This girl!" (Pointing at myself with both thumbs.)

He ignored me. "There are very few nerve endings in the cervix."

At this point I interrupted him by having a minor apoplectic seizure. The first through sixth words out of my mouth were, "Aack fuckgack dahshit whodya woah dat." I startled myself back to reality when I snapped my pencil in half. Oh, now I really hated him.

Um, really? That's the story you're sticking with, Dr. Dickhead? It's not going to hurt? You're going to say this to a woman who just had a bunch of chunks taken out of her cervix and knows a thing or two about nerve endings that may or may not be found there, yet you're going to tell her about how the cervix can't feel pain? Is this supposed to be some kind of Jedi mind trick? Because if so, I'm immune to your powers, old man. Do YOU have a cervix, Sir? And has anyone recently used a laser to burn off a piece of it?

I wasn't having any of it. He was going to knock me out, or I was going to knock him out. (I would, however, assure him first that there are very few nerve endings in the scrotum, and I'd even let him hold the nurse's hand while I used *a laser* on his jingle bells.)

I was most emphatically *not* going to be awake for the conization. History tells me that medical procedures are never as easy-peazy-lemon-squeezy as doctors want you to believe, regardless of how many times they promise that it'll be over in a jiffy. (A "jiffy" is a unit of time used by doctors that roughly equates to between 65 and 125 minutes. It was first used by a secretary in 1954 to describe the amount of time between your scheduled appointment and when you actually got to see the doctor. #TrueStory)

So, cut back to me, with a furious look on my face. I knew he was lying about the no-pain part (I'd just had biopsies taken, after all). But also, at that time in my life, I'd started suffering from severe panic attacks that had begun in grad school, when I was working full-time during the day and going to school full-time at night. I was under a lot of stress, which made it a highly inconvenient time to start having panic attacks.

If you've never had a panic attack, you're missing out on a sphincter-clenching delight. I'd describe the terror of a panic attack almost exactly the same way I'd describe that feeling you get just before massively shitting yourself in public (or so I hear). This very visceral fright is often accompanied by scary thoughts, like the fear of an oncoming wave of shame and humiliation when you realize the fiery launch in your skivvies will begin in T minus 30 seconds, while the nearest bathroom is T minus 60 seconds away. When I have a panic attack, my mind races and amplifies all of my unsettling thoughts. I sometimes curse my evolved *Homo sapien* brain and wish I had the brain of a slug.[74] Honestly, what has an awareness of my own existence ever done for me? Wouldn't it be nice to have thoughts no deeper than, "My, isn't this a lovely damp area? Oh, look! Lichen!"

Slugs never worry about their own mortality. I doubt they go around thinking, "Cheesus, what if someone pours salt on me today?"

If they did, they'd all carry around a shell to retreat into, like those nervous Nellies, the snails.[75] Slugs don't give any fucks, and

---

[74] I'd appreciate it if you'd keep your jokes about how I already have the brain of a slug to yourselves. Athankya.

[75] I think a nervous snail might be my spirit animal. I wish I had a shell I could hide in whenever I run into someone I know at the grocery store.

what a lovely way to exist ... not putting judgmental labels on every-thing that happens. As a slug, I wouldn't be worrying about what others thought of me. I could even get slime on my shirt without immediately thinking, "Fuck, that hot slug I have a crush on, Fran, is going to see this stain and think I'm incapable of taking care of myself. Dammit. Now I'll probably end up with 'Wonky Willy,' that guy with the busted antenna."

Unlike most people, slugs simply *exist* in a world where events are neither good nor bad. They're like tiny Zen masters, or Keanu Reeves in *Bill & Ted's Excellent Adventure*. They aren't even freaked out about being covered in mucus. (I wouldn't be caught dead in public if I was all clammy.)

I'm the opposite of Zen. And I **leap to delusions** all the time, which is exactly the problem with having a more developed brain. My first panic attack lasted for hours because I had an itch inside my ear that I couldn't scratch. I thought it'd never go away. Then I thought it would literally drive me insane, and I'd have to be com-mitted and put in a tiny padded cell. I got to thinking about how I'd only be given a plastic spoon to eat with, because I wouldn't be trusted with a plastic fork. It's impossible to eat spaghetti with a spoon, and I really like spaghetti. So there I'd be, stuck in a padded cell with spaghetti stains down the front of my all-white, insane-asy-lum jumpsuit, and how is that going to look when the psychiatrist comes to talk with me? She'd never let me out. Is it any wonder I was having a panic attack? Heh, so tell me again what's so great about sentience? Sure, I can explore the meaning of life and share it on Twitter using 140 character or less, but other than that, it only leads to marinara stains and permanent isolation.

My panic attacks generally start with a mild concern over some inconsequential problem. Then I build up a scenario in my mind that gets scarier and scarier, until it reaches its most outlandish (inevitable) conclusion. Take, for example, when I'm about to get on an elevator. If there's not enough room for all the occupants to lie down without needing to take turns, I won't get on. 'Cause what if the building loses power? What if it loses power due to a giant storm, and the entire area loses power for days? It could take weeks before the utility company fixes the power, because our building would likely be at the very end of the power grid. I'd be stuck in the elevator for months with all these strangers, and at some point, I'd need to take a shit in a corner, only there wouldn't be an unoccupied corner, because we packed ourselves in like a bunch of asshats in a big fucking hurry to get to a different floor. I'd be kicking myself for not waiting, and all the other occupants would be pissed at me, because we'd only have been trapped for five minutes, and already I'm taking a dump in the middle of the elevator. Then we'd lose the backup lights and be stuck in the dark in an elevator that smells like poo. Someone would lose his mind (probably one of the guys who works in accounting—those germophobes) and start freaking out (it's not my fault he got poo on his hand; he shouldn't have been touching me), and he'd start killing every person in the elevator, one by one, until I'd be the only one left. When we'd finally be rescued (after twenty minutes), he'd tell the rescuers I was the killer, and they'd believe him, because I'd have shit dripping down my leg, and I'd be so frazzled that I'd look exactly like the type of person who might have gone crazy in an elevator and killed all the other occupants. The headline would be: "Frazzled Female Freaks Out over Fecal Matter and Snuffs Fellow Passengers." Fran would have to divorce me after that. He'd probably change his name, too, so I couldn't find him.[76]

---

[76] Sorry for that really long paragraph, but once my mind starts going, there are no breaks.

At times, it can be helpful to work out scenarios to their ridiculous conclusions like this. Then I can laugh at myself, and think, that's silly ... what are the chances that I'll shit in the elevator and some madman will try to kill me? (You might try this if you suffer from anxiety.) Then I'll be able to get on the elevator. Except that seconds later, my stomach will start to rumble and I'll realize how incredibly realistic the scenario was, and for the entire panic-filled ride, I'll berate myself for not taking the fucking stairs. And by the way, during a panic attack, time slows down, so the elevator ride would take thirteen and a half years. It's physics. (Maybe forget what I just said about taking scenarios to their ridiculous conclusions. It never works.)

For me, any feeling of being trapped can cause a panic attack. Being in a situation I can't easily escape from (like being on an airplane, or in an MRI machine, or talking to people) can cause me to begin to panic. I knew with certainty that I was going to feel trapped during the entire cervical conization. Simply having the Jaws of Life (speculum) cranking open my vajayjay, and keeping it open for an hour, is not how I usually like to spend an afternoon.[77] I could be stuck on the table for an indeterminable length of time if things went sideways. There was no question I'd feel terribly confined while also in the throes of a panic attack.

Here's one possible scenario: Two seconds into the conization, I'd start worrying that I needed to fart. Then, because it's impossible to clench with your legs spread apart, I'd worry I wouldn't be able to

---

[77] By the way, why do gynecologists still use speculums? The speculum was invented by ancient Greeks, fer fuck's sake. And seriously? In all this time, no one could come up with anything less intrusive? You'll notice when it came to shoving something up a man's rectum for a look-see (colonoscopy), the invention of a thin wire with a very tiny camera certainly got fast-tracked.

hold it in. And what if I let one rip just as the surgeon bent over for a closer examination? That would be mortifying. But worse, what if, from sheer embarrassment, my sphincter completely betrays me, and instead of a fart, I shart? What if I take a giant, exploding shit right in the doctor's face?[78] Surely one of the nurses will have a smartphone, and she'd sell the photos to some tabloid, like the *Weekly World News*. My face would be in all the papers with a headline that reads, "Shart Shooter Kills Doctor When Ass Detonates." I'd never be able to show my face in public again, and Fran would move out, because who wants to be married to the woman who sharted so hard she killed someone? Why put himself in the danger zone? Is there such a thing as asshicular manslaughter? There would be now. They'd call it "Karen's Law," and it would garner bipartisan support.

Okay, maybe it *was* unlikely that anyone would actually die during the procedure, but it was *very* possible it would take a lot longer than the doctor said. If I started to have a panic attack in the middle of the procedure, would the doctor let me take a break? Knowing Dr. Pompousass (like I did), I didn't think so. And how humiliating to have to ask for a time-out in the middle of a conization. Once I'd interrupted His Holiness, it was very unlikely I'd ever agree to let him continue, anyway. Then the *News at 11* would be, "Hysterical Woman Fears Taking a Shit on Surgeon, Refuses Further Treatment." And there would be a video clip of me with a voice-over from the newscaster, saying, "... last seen crying in a Dairy Queen parking lot, eating her third Blizzard."

I simply knew I didn't want to be awake if things took an ugly turn. It would be best for everyone involved if the doctor just

---

[78] I don't know why my mind usually goes right to an embarrassing scenario involving shit, but it does.

knocked me the fuck out and woke me up when it was all over.

Dr. Pompousass kept insisting he'd do the procedure in his office, though. My discussion with him had turned into *a Mexican handoff.* No way was I going to go through this while awake. Not for *all the tea in Carolina.* Ultimately, I guess Dr. Pompousass realized I wasn't going to cave (that is *not* a euphemism for my vagina), and he finally agreed to knock me out, but he was incredibly disdainful about the whole idea. Looking back, I don't even know why I agreed to let this asshole perform the surgery. I guess I was young, scared, and just wanted to get it over with as soon as possible.

On the day of the procedure, Dr. Pompousass stopped by as I was waiting to go in for surgery and asked how I was doing. I said, "I'm very nervous."

He smirked and said something along the lines of, "I guess so! Since you're going under anesthesia for *no* reason."

Or words to that effect. What a condescending shit. And right before I went under the knife. Way to make me feel like I'm in good hands, dick.

When Lola saw my drawing of the colposcope, she told me about her experience. She had a LEEP procedure done, (Loop Electrosurgical Excision Procedure), which is similar to a laser conization, only it's done using an electrified wire loop to burn out the abnormal tissue on the cervix. Lola remembered smoke coming out of her vagina. Seriously. Here's what she wrote:

> My gynosadist offered to do the procedure under general anesthesia in the hospital, but on the phone to schedule it, her nurse made it sound like only weenie-women opt for general anesthesia, and I was kind of John Wayne (with a vagina) back then, so I said I'd do it in the office with local anesthetic. Because, yanno, I had things to do. O_o

As it turned out, this was a grave mistake on my part, because the local anesthetic didn't work. At all.

I'm. Not. Kidding.

I felt everything. Ever-y-thing. And it felt pretty much like my gynosadist was BRANDING MY CERVIX REPEATEDLY LIKE I WAS A COW AND I'M NOT KIDDING.

I was clutching the back of the table with my hands over my head while sweating profusely, all the while thinking it was supposed to hurt like that, because ... after all ... childbirth had hurt kind of like that and nobody said anything about it. (Well, they said, "Are you feeling any discomfort?" until I killed them.) But yeah, I assumed it was supposed to hurt like that.

Afterward, I cried like a little kid (NOT kidding). My gynosadist said that, usually, when people hurt like that, they "jump around on the table." (*I'm not kidding.* That's what she said. For fuck's sake.) So *I* said, "It seemed to me (at the time) that 'jumping around the table' might have resulted in ... oh, I dunno ... your *hot poker piercing my vagina, burrowing through my esophagus, and emerging out of my throat, you homicidal maniac!*"

I didn't say the homicidal-maniac part, but only because I was too busy weeping.

It was seriously the single most painful medical procedure I've ever endured. I decided right then that I would never, ever allow another person to *set fire to my cervix* again.

I'm delighted to say that I've kept that promise. Go me.

I wrote back: My cervix (what's left of it) sends your cervix her regards.

My understanding is that there are three methods for doing a cervical cone biopsy. LEEP (which I think is the one Lola had), cold knife (a scalpel), and laser (using a carbon dioxide laser to burn away tissue, though "burn away" may not be the technical term). I found out later that a laser conization is not only a more time-consuming and expensive procedure (I guess Dr. Pompousass needed a new Ferrari), but it also has a significant drawback when compared to the cold-knife conization. The problem is the tissue around the biopsy site is changed by the heat from the laser (or the wire loop, in the case of LEEP).[79] This means the lab can't always thoroughly "check the margins." With a cold knife, on the other hand, they can easily evaluate all of the tissue around the biopsy to look for cancer cells, which is, again, made more difficult with a laser or LEEP biopsy.

The National Institute of Health website has a study of these three methods of cervical conization: LEEP, cold knife, and laser. (I believe the authors are: P. Mathevet, D. Dargent, M. Roy, and G. Beau.)[80] According to the copyright on the site, the information appears to be in the public domain, so I'll quote a portion of the abstract here (if I end up in jail for this, I'll be needing a pen pal. And someone to bake me a cupcake with a chainsaw in it):

> "These results suggest that in our hands: (1) laser conization is relatively costly and time consuming and alters the tissues significantly, and (2) the choice between cold knife

---

[79] And yeah, that "more time consuming" part really pissed me off, considering Dr. Pompousass wanted me to be awake the entire time! What a douche.

[80] http://www.ncbi.nlm.nih.gov/pubmed/8063242

and LEEP is more difficult—cold knife gives a sample adequate for histological evaluation (including evaluation of the margins), while the LEEP procedure is technically easier and less time consuming but sometimes induces electrocautery artifact so that evaluation of the margins is not possible."

So my story checks out: Dr. Pompousass was a greedy, self-righteous prick. Because what the actual fuck? He didn't want to be sure he got all the fucking cancer and/or precancerous cells? Wasn't that the whole point of the procedure? Instead, he chose the most expensive and time-consuming method of cervical mutilation.

Bitter? Who, me? (Yup.) I remember asking him later about the biopsy results. He told me there was no biopsy. He said he had, "Burned away the suspicious areas."

Motherf—! He thought it was okay to blast my cervix with a lightsaber without making sure he got all the cancer? Fucking moron. I hope he all but dies from testicular cancer because his doctor decided to use a hot match head, like he was removing a tick instead of cancer, in case Dr. Pompousass wanted to have a kid later. Because ***what's good for the goose is good for the salamander.***

The moral of the story is to do your homework and don't get bullied into a particular treatment method by your doctor, so you don't regret it later. Alternatively, the moral of the story is don't read studies *after* you've had a procedure done.

How many bad cliches has it been? I've lost count. And also, my liver just broke up with me. Said it wasn't working out between us. But even my butt thinks my liver is being an asshole.[81] There may

---

[81] I hope you saw what I did there.

be a third moral: playing drinking games is stupid. I hope I'm the only one who made *that* mistake.

Let's just say that I love doctors as much as I love taking a shit in a public toilet, which is to say, not at all

NOTE: I REALIZE 5.5 is an absurd number for a book chapter, but I wrote it after I wrote chapters 6 through 14 and was too fuckin' lazy to re-number them all, so this is where we are now.

In case you haven't noticed, I don't much like doctors. On my long list of People I Don't Like, doctors are right up there, between serial-killer rapists and people who pronounce pecan, "pee-can."[82] Here's another story about a doctor's visit to further help illustrate why I find most of these fuckers annoying.

A couple years ago, I woke up and the room was spinning—and not in that "oh-this-is-fun-I'm-still-drunk" kind of way—it was more of a "holy-shit-pass-me-a-bucket" kind of way. Fran drove me to our doctor's office and—since my usual, compassionate general

---

[82] And also, anyone who pronounced potato "po-tah-to" can go fuck themselves.

practitioner, Dr. Fein, wasn't available—I had an appointment with one of the asshats at her practice. I won't call him Dr. Asshole, because that would be uncouth, and you know how much I fuckin' hate vulgar language. But also, I wouldn't want you to mistakenly have the impression that he was one of those endearing assholes, like George Costanza on *Seinfeld* or Arthur Spooner on *King of Queens*. Instead, I'll call him Dr. Lecter.

Before I met with Dr. Lecter, I spoke to a nurse. The first question the nurse asked me was, "What brings you in today?"

I said, "I woke up this morning, laying on my right side, then rolled over to my left side to turn off the alarm clock, and the room started spinning, so I think I have benign paroxysmal positional vertigo."

Medical folks hate it when patients self-diagnose, but we can't help it, can we?

She busily typed all of this into a laptop, and said nothing. Probably depressed/pissed because an idiot like me can go on WebMD.com and do her job; meanwhile, she's probably still paying off her nursing school loans.

I said, "I had trouble walking to the bathroom and felt very nauseous and motion sick."

She nodded and continued typing. I added, "My husband had vertigo last year, and part of his treatment involved the doctor manipulating his head around, rather abruptly, into various positions. I'd just like to remind the doctor that I have a herniated disc in my neck, so I'd rather there be no head jerking of any sort, please." Or words to that effect.

I bet medical folks really *really* hate it when you tell them about someone you know who had your symptoms, or even worse, when you tell them exactly how you'd like your self-diagnosed ailment to be treated. And those "Ask your doctor if X is right for you" commercials probably make them want to punch themselves in the face. The nurse continued typing on her laptop, then took my blood pressure and left me to wait for the doctor.

After about fifteen minutes, Dr. Lecter (who would undoubtedly prefer to be called "God") rapped on the door twice and walked in. He didn't even wait for me to say "enter" before barging in, which would have been awkward if He'd caught me doing something stupid, like trying to hack into the laptop the nurse left behind. But I didn't hack into the laptop, because whatever that nurse wrote on my chart was most likely medical jargon that I wouldn't understand anyway.[83] My first impression of God was that He appeared to be an asshole. Turns out, I nailed it. He looked like a cross between Mr. Smithers from *The Simpsons* and Mrs. Oleson from *Little House on the Prairie*. He oozed contempt. God mumbled, "Hello," without making eye contact, and He immediately logged in and began to read something on the laptop the nurse had left behind.

God then asked, "So what brings you in today?"

Maybe God didn't understand medical jargon either? No, I quite prudently assumed God had read the nurse's notes, and He just wanted me to quickly confirm what she wrote. So, not wanting to waste any of His time (God is pretty important, after all, and must be so busy between the healing and the prayer answering that He barely has time to Netflix and chill), I simply replied, "Dizziness," without elaborating. I even carefully avoided using the word "vertigo," figuring I should wait for God's judgment.

God said, "Well, you know, *dizziness* is pretty vague. It can

---

[83] Plus, the password was not "password," "PASSWORD," or "pa$$w0rd," so I quickly gave up in the face of their impressively sophisticated security precautions.

mean a lot of different things. Tell me *exactly* what happened and what you felt."

Well, okay ... so now I was thinking maybe the nurse was just fucking off and didn't write down anything I'd told her. Or maybe God didn't read her notes at all and was just checking His email (or Mary and Joseph fan-fiction porn?), so I started telling Him my story again, from the beginning.

"I woke up this morning, was laying on my right side, then rolled over to my left side to turn off the alarm clock, and the room started spinning. I had trouble walking to the bathroom ... " yada yada yada. Then I said, 'cause I *knew* he hadn't read the nurse's notes, "I'm sure it's all in my records, but I just want to mention that, if I do have vertigo, my husband had it recently and told me part of the treatment involved head and neck manipulation ..." Aaaaaaand, right there, God cut me off.

He seemed somewhat annoyed when He said, "Yeah, I know, I know. I've got all the nurse's notes right here."

Ummmm, you have what now? (Charming guy, God.)

Why was He asking me to repeat the whole fucking story about how I came to be dizzy if He had all the nurse's notes right there? Was this some kind of test? Was He trying to catch me in a lie so He could smite me? Lying is like, some kind of abomination, right? Maybe He thought I was an abominator.

I was a little insulted. I may have 99 problems, but being an abominator isn't one of them. I shut my pie hole before I could say, "Well, ex-cuuuuse me," because I figured there was no use arguing with God.

So God moves on and decides to do a quick neurological exam.

God said, "Squeeze my fingers.... Now push up against my hands.... Now push down...."

But He did this all *really* fast. I mean, *boom boom boom* ... do this ... now do that.... I had trouble keeping up with God's commands, because He was going through them so quickly.

Mind you, I get very nervous when I'm in a doctor's office, as They of the White-Coated Profession scare the crap out of me, so I was already more than a little rattled, but now I'm thinking, why a neurologic exam? What medical condition, besides an inner ear problem, can cause dizziness? Is He trying to rule out an inoperable brain tumor? Shit! Does brain cancer also give you the tremors? 'Cause now my hands were starting to shake. I hope He's only checking to see if I'm a demon-possessed abomination.

God then held out His finger, in front of my eyes and said, "Touch your nose, then touch my finger."

I complied.

God then moved His finger to the left and again said, "Touch your nose, then my finger."

He kept moving His finger around to different points in space, but He did this very quickly, as if the insurance company would give Him a bonus for every time I touched His finger. It started to feel like a game of "Simon Says" that was going horribly wrong. Or maybe it was more like the children's game "monkey in the middle," only there was just the two of us, and I was clearly the monkey. He began moving His finger around so fast that I was sure He was just trying to trip me up. So I slapped Him.

Well, okay, I didn't slap Him, but I should have, because inoperable brain tumors probably make your uncontrollable slapping reflex go into overdrive. I concentrated a little harder, but since God always wins, I dejectedly began to wonder why I should bother. At one point, I accidentally touched His finger first, then touched my nose, which was completely backwards (to my great shame, I had fallen short in the eyes of the Lord), and He became downright derisive: "Noooo ... I *said*, 'Touch your nose, *then* touch my finger!'"

(God really said this to me. And in the tone of voice you'd use when explaining to your parents for the bajillionth time how to use their new cell phone. "You have to hit the green button to pick up, *not* the red one," only meaner.) God obviously has a God complex.

So yikes!!! Apparently, I had displeased God. Lesson learned: Follow God's commandments, or suffer His wrath.

Next, God told me to open my mouth, and He shined a light into it. He then shined the light up my nose. Now I'm thinking He's checking for ear, nose, and throat cancer. Will He need to remove half my face if I have cancer of the sinuses? Will I end up looking like Voldemort? Or worse, Michael Jackson? At this point, God is looking for what is likely a brain tumor so large that it's visible by looking up my nose.

He never expressly told me I could shut my mouth, so to avoid being chastised again for failing to follow His directions to the letter, I left my mouth dutifully hanging open while God continued to examine me. That's when He said, "You can close your mouth now. You look kind of silly."

I shit you not. That's a direct quote from God's lips to my ears. "You look kind of silly." God made fun of me for leaving my mouth open. Who knew God was such a fucking bully?[84]

A bit stunned and embarrassed, I said, "Oh, sorry, yes, I guess I do look silly."

Well, He must have taken pity on me, having discerned that He was dealing with a frightened moron, and He said, "Oh, that's okay."

That's okay, He tells me?! What an enormous relief! God told

---

[84] Well, I guess everyone in Egypt who suffered from the ten plagues knew. And all those men, women, and children who died in that flood. That was pretty dickish. Why couldn't He have just given them all wedgies?

me I didn't need to apologize for looking silly! Wasn't that thoughtful of Him? I guess, sometimes, He truly can be a loving God. (What an infuriating turd goblin.)

Can you believe it? I didn't get an "I was only joking." Nope, nothing like that. I just got an implied, "It's okay that you look silly. You can't help it. Plus, I'm a just and merciful God. I know in your heart you're repentant about how stupid you look, so I forgive you."

Dr. Lecter. The Patron Saint of Douchebaggery.

And here's another thing that had me fuming: He started writing a prescription for some motion-sickness medicine called meclizine, so I asked Him if I could just take some Dramamine, because it's over-the-counter and I've used it loads of times when I fly or, occasionally, when riding in a car, and my insurance doesn't include prescription drug coverage. He said, "You could, but I'd rather you take this." (See drawing below.)

In the beginning God created a prescription pad. The pad was void and without signature. And at the end of the sixth day, God said, "Let there be drugs," and there were drugs. God saw that the drugs were good.

(This might explain why God rested on the seventh day. Stoners can be so lazy.)

Oh, you'd rather I take this, would you? Getting a little kick-back from a pharmaceutical company, are we? You want me to pay three times more for this fucking prescription than I'd pay if I just bought an over-the-counter medicine that would do exactly the same thing? Fuck that. So, as soon as I left, I went to the pharmacy to fill His prescription for Meclizine.

What? I told you doctors scare me.

Still, I sometimes feel guilty about following their orders. Like I'm enabling doctors by reinforcing their God delusions when I obey their every command. One of these days, I'm going to stand up to a God, and tell Him,[85] "NO! Damn You! I will *not* touch my finger to my nose and then to Your finger. I will touch my finger to *Your* finger and then to *my* nose ... or touch my nose twice, then touch Your finger ... and maybe I'll even tap Your forehead a few times while I'm at it. I might even make use of my free will and start poking You in the chest because I don't have to do whatever You say. How do You like them apples? And speaking of apples, fuck You! That's right, I said fuck You, God. Of *course* Eve ate the apple. Apples are delicious, Asshole. You should have made the tree of knowledge a round prickly cactus if it was so goddamned important nobody eat from it." But I'll probably just mutter all this under my breath and then He'll send me for a psychiatric evaluation.

And I'll go.

---

[85] I've found this problem typically occurs mostly with male doctors.

Chapter 6

Unreasonably aggressive boob acupuncture

G ETTING BACK TO MY boob ... the wait was finally over. The day arrived in early January, when I was scheduled to have a partial boob amputation via chainsaw (a core needle biopsy). So far, 2014 was shaping up to be the Best. Year. Evah!

By the way, here comes some of the "violence" I warned you about in the addendum. I hope everybody read the addendum first. It contains a warning. If you haven't read it yet, you might want to take a look now, before continuing. We can wait.

J/K (see "old ass"); we're not waiting. Here, I'll summarize it for you, "There will be cursing ... blah blah blah ... there will be some political incorrectness ... blahditty blah blah." Now, let's get right into the boob acupuncture.

First, a couple of nurses (I guess they were nurses—they could

have been janitors, for all I know, or random boobarazzi who regularly crash boobie-biopsy parties[86]) had me lie down on my stomach
on a cold table that had at *least* a millimeter of padding—possibly
two. So plush. Like it was designed for comfort. (If the person you
designed the table for was that asshole driver who wouldn't let you
merge, but you felt like a bed of nails would have been a bit much.
That level of comfort.) Thankfully, though, I was given one of those
lovely salmon-colored hospital gowns I'm so fond of. (I'm an au-
tumn, so the color really works with my complexion.)

So these boobarazzi had me lie facedown on the hydraulic-lift,
metal table. I needed a stepping stool to climb onto it, even though
it looked like the table could have been raised while I was on it, like
a car in an auto-body shop. Was the step ladder an insult? I bet if I
was a skinny supermodel they would have used the hydraulics to el-
evate it, but in my case, they decided to spare the wear and tear on
their table's motor.

My boob dropped through a hole in the table, where it was gently crushed by ... I'm not exactly what, since I couldn't see. I assume
it was the mammogram machine my doctor warned me about, but
it felt like a giant boob hug—a hug that was to boobs what Lennie
from *Of Mice and Men* was to bunnies. That squeeze made me feel
warm and safe, like a baby seal at a party for hungry polar bears. Plus,
I appreciated the two-fer special: buy one torture, get the second one
free.

The doctor lowered the table a tad, and since I hadn't paid attention to the mechanics of it, I wondered if instead of hydraulics
there might be a mini forklift in the room. Was it being operated by
a little person—or, as my husband would say, a "smidget"? (Side

---

[86] These same people probably like to attend routine Pap smears, as well.
Is that where the word paparazzi came from? Wouldn't surprise me.

note: Fran and I refer to everyone in his mom's family as smidgets, because they're all about five feet tall and under. That sounds terrible, but when you consider that some of our alternative names for them have included "Oompa Loompas" and "munchkins," I think you'll agree "smidget" isn't all that bad.[87]

My mother-in-law says she's the youngest of eleven kids, but I'm sure there were more. Probably lost a few in crowds or from slipping through sewer grates. How could they not, when they're all so goddamned tiny? Still, Fran knows it's a horrible thing to call short people "smidgets," so we only call them that behind their backs. It's called being polite, because if you can't say something nice, say it out of earshot.)[88] And dammit. On top of all my other offensive bullshit, let's add heightist to the heap.[89] I'm like the Archie Bunker of Generation X.

Looking back, I don't actually believe the table was being raised and lowered by a really short forklift driver, but I was on Xanax, so I can't be 100% sure. Plus, I kind of hope it was Peter Dinklage. He's a pretty hawt smidget.

Because of my bad neck, I had my head turned toward the right

---

[87] It really is that bad. At least I'll have a roommate in hell.

[88] Plus they're right at ball-height, so Fran needs to be careful.

[89] Truth be told, I would have killed to be a little person. I was unusually self-conscious in middle school (*I know! I'm like a solitary, tragic snowflake*), since I was taller than most of the boys and all but one of the girls. By sixth grade, I had adopted the tall-girl-slouch in a misguided attempt to trick boys into thinking I was shorter and therefore more dateable. Thankfully, my growth spurt stopped just shy of five feet eight while I was in high school, or I'd have become a social outcast. Then I'd have dropped out of school and become one of those tall, dancing-noodle guys that you see in auto dealership lots, because what else was I going to do?

(it's uncomfortable for me to turn my head very far in either direction, but if I have to choose one, it hurts less if I turn toward the right), which happened to be facing the wall. So when my surgeon, Dr. Cutter, came in, I blindly wiggled some fingers at her in a greeting. I'm pretty sure she waved back. I was particularly glad she couldn't see my face, as it was smashed into the table, and I probably looked like a flounder doing "**duck lips**" (see "old ass"), anyway. Socially awkward greeting avoided! Yay, me!

Dr. Cutter asked how I was doing. Pfft ... how the fuck did she *think* I was doing? I was half-naked, staring at a wall, lying on a cold, uncomfortable table with my tit dangling through a hole, held by a vise grip on the other side. I cheerily replied, "I'm doing well. How are you?"

I truly wanted to know how she was doing. If she'd had a bad morning, it might interfere with her concentration on the task at hand. She told me she was doing great! (She definitely ended her response with an exclamation point.) But instead of making me feel better, this concerned me. What kind of sadistic asshat gets excited when they're about to slice into someone's breast? Paging Dr. Torquemada: your next victim is ready. Or maybe she'd just gotten back from a particularly satisfying kill during a Doctors Without Borders trip. She was a bit happy-clappy. The forecast for the day's procedure went from partly sunny to cloudy with a chance of holy shit.

She got down to business, manipulating my boob while Peter Dinklage adjusted the table height, until she found the perfect boob-flattening setting on the mammogram equipment. Then she gave me a shot of Lidocaine, or Novocaine, or Candycaine. A couple of minutes later, she stood up, touched me lightly on the back with both hands, and told me I would hear a "pop," but to try to remain still, which was actually quite easy to do, since my left boob was clamped down like it was in the mouth of a crocodile with lockjaw.

I was in no position to go anywhere. I have no idea what made her think I could, unless she thought I might leap off the table and run screaming out of the room, leaving my left tit behind.

I guessed the popping sound was the machine pushing the core needle into my breast, rather than the sound of a gun being fired in celebration of the boobarazzi absconding with a piece of my tit (but again, I was staring at the wall, soooo ... who knows?).

The surgeon spent forever poking around in my boob. The procedure wasn't horribly painful (thanks to the anesthetic) so much as it was horribly unpleasant. It began with aggressive tugging before escalating to what was almost a disagreeable pinching sensation, before proceeding to being a disagreeable pinching sensation.

All the while, the parts of my body around the table's boob-hole, like my ribcage and the area just below my shoulder, rubbed aggressively against the barely padded metal surface. After a few minutes, Dr. Cutter had obtained her first chunk of my breast, which, I later learned, she was able to examine on a computer screen, using x-ray equipment that had been set up in the room. This allowed her to check the biopsied sample and make sure it contained the microcalcifications she was targeting.

Not completely satisfied that the first sample got all of the tissue she wanted, Dr. Cutter commenced to hacking into my boob even more. After each hack, she carried the sample over to the computer to x-ray it. By the 300th (or third) sample, there was an extended conversation among the boobarazzi, as they huddled around the computer screen five feet away. They were discussing whether or not they should obtain tissue from yet another area, where they could see shadows (or invasive breast cancer?) on the mammogram image. Dr. Cutter then turned her attention back to my boob. She dug around like a toddler with his finger up his nose, grabbed yet another sample (*POP!*), then mumbled something about it being "enough" and not wanting to "go too far."

Say what now? Time out! Flag on the play! What exactly do you mean by "go too far"? Sweet Cheesus, is my nipple in danger of being skewered by your biopsy needle? Hello! I can hear everything you're saying!

I think Dr. Cutter took four biopsies, but I don't recall exactly. After three hours (or forty-five minutes) she released the boob clamp and had me slowly sit up. She then asked me to hold and apply pressure to a gauze pad she had placed over the bleeding incision, while she went to get a couple of butterfly bandages. Ummm ... shouldn't holding the gauze pad have been *her* job? I'm sorry you hate your job, but I'm not trained to hold gauze pads! Besides, I'm sure one of the boobarazzi would have been thrilled to do it. Christ Almighty, I'm surprised she didn't just hand me the scalpel, point, and say, "Cut here."

After the procedure, Dr. Cutter commented on how relaxed I seemed. "See?" she said. "That wasn't too bad, was it?"

She was either under the false impression that I was hella brave, or she was angling for a positive review on **Yelp** (see "old ass").

I confessed that I'd taken a Xanax earlier. She looked slightly disappointed, turned away, and said, unenthusiastically, "Oh, that was a good idea. Probably everyone should take a Xanax beforehand."

Well, chyaaaa! 'Cause your fuckin' extra-awesome humungous titty acupuncture machine ... designed to both crush *and* shove a large probing metal arm violently into a breast, frankly scares the shit out of people! And what's with that fucking *popping sound?* Why did the entire table shake when the probe was shot into my boob? For as much as you're charging for this procedure, I'm sure you could afford a table that doesn't wobble. Where else have you been cutting costs? Are you going to rub my boob with some Aspercreme for pain relief instead of injecting it with Lidocaine? Forget the Xanax. How about giving patients a horse tranquilizer beforehand?

The only reason I wasn't trembling like a mouse in a snake's terrarium was because I had taken Xanax. As it was, I trembled (like a bowl of Jell-O) only when touched. To be clear, I am careful not to abuse Xanax. I take it only before situations when I know I'm going to be particularly stressed out, like flying, going to the dentist, or having a piece of my tit removed. I'm not a fan of taking drugs, and I don't think it's a good idea to take a psychoactive drug like Xanax on a daily basis to help reduce anxiety. I have booze for that.

I suppose everyone experiences anxiety differently. Mine often arises in the form of "black and white" or "what if" thinking. As an example, hours after the procedure, when the Xanax wore off, I was back home and in the grips of panic again. I mentioned (bitched) earlier about how tightly the machine gripped my boob, but there was one point during the procedure when my breast may have slipped a little. I was supposed to keep my head turned to the right, but holding it there for so long was becoming intolerable. I lifted my chin off the table to try to turn my head to the left, and as I raised my head, I could feel my boob pull the tiniest bit out of the clamp. I didn't pull my entire boob out, but it definitely felt as though it had slipped ever-so-slightly from its original position.

The doctor more or less yelled at me to try not to move, so I quickly put my head back down, still turned uncomfortably to the right. I didn't worry about it too much at the time (because Xanax), but my anxiety caused me to obsess for hours after the procedure. My mind kept rehashing "the boob slippage incident," as I'd begun to refer to it, and I couldn't stop thinking, "Shit! I moved after the doctor had the needle perfectly positioned! Instead of grabbing the next suspicious looking tissue sample, she probably grabbed a sample of perfectly healthy breast tissue and missed my cancerous lesion by half a millimeter! OMG, they are going to think I'm cancer free when I'm not! I am soooo going to die...."

As you can see, I'd managed to combine my "what if" thinking (what if the doctor missed the cancerous lesion because I moved my tit?) and my "black and white" thinking (that means she missed getting a biopsy of my spreading cancer!). Once my mind gets on a roll like this, it can take some time for me to turn it off.

That's how my anxious mind works. Further, I don't just worry that something bad *might* happen. I convince myself that something terrible is *definitely* going to happen (or has already happened) ... and now I'm going to die. Sometimes that means "to die" in the literal sense of ceasing to live, and that's what I mean in this case. At other times I mean "I'm going to die" in the sense of being horribly embarrassed. For example, I might worry that I will say or do something really humiliating and think, "I'll be so mortified, I'll die!"

But for clarification, I don't ever mean "die" or "died" in the way the kids use it these days ... as in: "OMG! That boy I have a crush on asked me out, and *I died ... I literally died!*" I don't mean it like that. (And why is it that kids don't understand what the word "literally" means?)

Eventually, I got over worrying about the slippage, because after the thousandth time of re-living the entire procedure in my head, I remembered that the doctor had x-rayed every tissue sample while I was on the table. This ensured that she had gotten a sample from each of the suspicious areas she saw on the mammogram. So thankfully, I finally got over the panic of receiving a "false negative" from the lab. Done with that foolishness, I turned my attention to the more practical task of panicking about how I was going to deal with my upcoming "true positive" result.

Of course testing positive for cancer wasn't the only thing I had been obsessing over, but thankfully, although my neck was quite sore afterward, the procedure didn't cause a major pain flare-up. As mentioned, this had been one of my biggest worries (next to dying or embarrassing myself). So at the end of the day, the core needle biopsy was not the *most* unrelaxing experience I'd ever had, but it was certainly in the top ten. (As a little kid, I once got motion sick on a carnival ride and threw up when it started spinning backwards. That was a top-ten unrelaxing experience for everyone involved.) But at least it was finally over. I had survived the procedure without crying or shitting myself, thank you very much. Not that I've ever actually shit myself during a medical procedure, but I wouldn't rule it out.[90] I was sore for the next few days (like Peter Dinklage had punched me in the tit repeatedly for referring to short people as smidgets), and I had a fair bit of bruising, but I was fine.

I considered having someone punch me in my right boob, so it would swell up to match the left one. Like breast enhancement, without silicone or surgery. (I should patent this shit. Sometimes I shock myself with my amazing ideas. Fran is always shocked by them, too. Just not in a good way.) As I mentioned, it was January, and a bitterly cold one at that, so it was especially unappealing to keep an ice pack on my poor, abused tit. Plus, I figured if I didn't ice it too much, I'd be a D-cup (instead of my usual C) for at least another twenty-four hours.

The next day, when Fran came home, I greeted him by standing at a distance with my hand on my hip, in full, voluptuous profile, with my bigger boob forward. He didn't even notice. Walked right

---

[90] I don't know why so many of my fears center on diarrhea. I feel like it's always a shit story with me. Have I thanked you, yet, for reading this book full of shitty stories? If not, I thank you.

by and crouched down to greet the dogs. When he is in the middle of greeting the dogs, I could light my hair on fire and Fran wouldn't notice. It's a five-minute, tail-wagging, licking love-fest every night when he comes home ... which could be fun, if only I were involved.

After going through this very stressful procedure, and while my boob was still black and blue and very sore (I wore a bra for support even while I slept, and I hate wearing bras), I was feeling a tad obsessed with what the results of the biopsy would be ... and, more specifically, how long I had to live. I started to wonder what I should ask Fran for. You know, as in, "You should get me [insert thing I always wanted] before I die from cancer!"

I needed to come up with something quick, in case I received good news about the biopsy on the following Monday.

I asked some friends if they had any ideas. One perceptive friend suggested I ask for some scented candles; another suggested I ask for a stress-relieving music CD.

I may need to distance myself from these people.

I was incredibly relieved the biopsy was over, but I felt a little like a new soldier after their first battle. Yes, I was still alive, but there were no guarantees on how long that would last. I was feeling fragile, vulnerable, and worn out. I was also terrified, but trying hard to avoid the embarrassment of letting it show. This is all extremely exhausting.

I of course clung to the hope that they'd tell me they found only benign calcifications, as expected, and that everything was just fine, since the alternative was that they'd found cancer. During the biopsy, Dr. Cutter said several times that she thought it was benign, and that she was erring on the side of caution because of my personal and family medical history. Well, isn't she a peach to make me go through this physical trauma for nothing? Was that supposed to make me feel better?

I know I'm being unreasonable. Dr. Cutter was simply doing her job, but as much as I wanted a clean bill of health, I also thought if she called on Monday to say things were benign, right after I got over my relief, I'd want to smack her. Really hard. And then maybe punch her in the tit.

Little did I know my results wouldn't be nearly as clear-cut as that, and I had a whole new type of nerve-racking procedure in store. < ------ Wait ... What? Is that another cliffhanger?

Fuck yeah. In your face, Dan Brown!

Chapter 7

A glimpse of my anxious mind, the results of the core needle biopsy, and the important things in life—like making a fortune before I die

I TRIED TO PREPARE mentally for possibly (assuredly) receiving bad news from the biopsy. This preparation was accomplished mostly through the clever use of internal dialogue, designed to trick myself into maintaining a positive outlook. Unfortunately, my optimistic attitude devolved back into despair in less time than it takes to burn toast.

Before I present an example of my internal discourse, I should give you a little glimpse of my crazy. Allow you to observe it, if you will, as if you were Dian Fossey and my mind was an 800-pound, anxious, and easily dejected gorilla.

Okay, so, this is some shit you'd witness if you were "in the mist." Believe it or not (and I wouldn't blame you if you didn't), I'm not *always* a fearful, insecure, self-loathing ninny. In fact, there are plenty of times when I'm feeling rather good about myself. Maybe even very nearly proud of some small accomplishment, like perhaps I've finished an oil painting I'm fairly happy with, or completed a sketch I don't hate. During those times, I actually feel damn near cheerful. I might even reminisce about that one time I successfully flipped a fried egg without breaking the yoke. A very proud moment. But invariably, right in the middle of that happy recollection, I'll remind myself of a time when I said or did something particularly stupid ... aaaand I'm right back to self-loathing. In thirty seconds or less, I can go from feeling somewhat satisfied to berating myself for being an especially appalling asshat. (See illustration of the process below.)

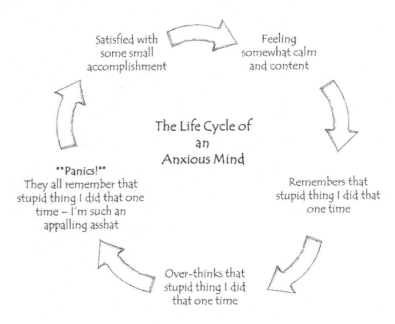

Satisfied with some small accomplishment

Feeling somewhat calm and content

The Life Cycle of an Anxious Mind

Remembers that stupid thing I did that one time

Over-thinks that stupid thing I did that one time

Panics!
They all remember that stupid thing I did that one time – I'm such an appalling asshat

Similarly, I was going round and round between optimism and pessimism while waiting for my biopsy results. I'd try to be confident and hope the results would be positive, but the next minute, I'd be scared shitless. Partly, this was because I'd start to wonder if it was such a good idea to hope for positive results. Maybe I should be hoping for negative results, as in the biopsy was *negative for cancer*? Shit! What if I'd put my intentions for positive results out into the Universe, and the Universe gave me exactly what I wanted, just like *The Secret* said it would? What if I'd *asked* the Universe to give me cancer, and it did?

So then I'd think, great, now I gave myself invasive breast cancer with my thoughts. And I'd start brooding again. I looked up some inspiring quotes, like this one from Socrates:

> "The secret of happiness, you see, is not found in seeking
> more, but in developing the capacity to enjoy less."

Well, that sounds pretty good. I get it. Like, don't wish for a new car to make you happy, just learn to be more content with the shitbox you already have. After all, there are probably a few folks in the world driving a donkey to work who *wish* they had a shitbox. Donkeys don't even have power steering or air conditioning. I should be happy I don't have to drive a shitbox donkey that's hot and hard to steer.

Or maybe, in my case, this quote would mean, don't seek *not* to have cancer, but develop a capacity for joy even if you have it, which is really an excellent way to look at things, Socrates. Man, you should have been, like, a philosopher or something.

On the other hand, what if by "developing the capacity to enjoy less," Socrates meant *literally* to try to enjoy less? As in "stop trying to be so fucking happy—you're making yourself miserable." Maybe being too happy makes the crappy times seem even crappier, and is it really possible to be cheery when life drops a big steaming turd on you? Maybe he's saying it's better to be less satisfied in general? Maybe we should be shooting for mildly content? Or even slightly depressed? I wish I knew what Socrates meant. I need more deets.[91] Honestly, dude, you may as well be speaking Greek. Does anyone know what the fuck you're going on about when you say, "developing the capacity to enjoy less"? Is that supposed to mean all the complaining assclowns of the world are the only ones doing joy right? If that's the case, hand me a crown and scepter, because I rule at belly-aching.

So, yeah, that's pretty much how I was flip-flopping between hope and gloom while waiting for my surgeon to call. It was also the middle of winter, and apropos of nothing: I'm not a fan. I live in Pennsylvania and hate it from January to the end of March.

To recap, we were about to go all *Gorillas in the Mist* on the daily workings of my mind leading up to the phone call from my surgeon. Here's one moment that would be a fair representation of a typical day: I was sitting in my chair wearing the t-shirt I'd slept in under a long-sleeved, thermal Henley, with a heavy flannel shirt on top of that. My clothes look like they were just shot out of a wrinkle gun. I had on fleece lounge pants with a snowman print and extra thick, "forty below" socks on top of crew socks.[92] I was also wearing a slouchy knit hat and fingerless gloves, because I'm always freezing,

---

[91] Is it just me or is it a bit ironic that kids are using the unspecific word "deets" for "details"? How is a listener supposed to know "deets" isn't short for "detachments," or "detainees," or even "dirty feet"? Wouldn't most people need more particulars to know what deets means? And why use it when we already have a fairly descriptive, detailed (if you'll pardon) word for details? It's called "details." Deets sounds more like something you'd call police detectives if you lived in Brooklyn. "Yo, Deets, whachu dooooin wit dat investigashin?" Oy. I should probably have turned my footnote rants into a separate novella.

[92] I like to imagine that my snowman-print lounge pants make me look adorably quirky, but they may, in fact, reveal that I'm a sad sack who drags ass all day while wearing glorified pajama bottoms.

even though Fran says *I'm* the one who told *him* where to set the thermostat, in order to be "environmentally conscious." (His argument makes no sense, so I continue to complain to him all winter about how cold the house is.) I'm fashion challenged. It's a chronic condition. So my inner dialogue went something like this (feel free to adapt this into a Broadway play, starring Zooey Deschanel as "Optimistic Me" and Bea Arthur as "Anxious Me," but maybe pick someone a little younger than Bea Arthur, because she's more than forty years older than I am, and also because it's probably hard to do a song and dance number when you're dead)[93]:

The curtain opens.

OPTIMISTIC ME: I'll bet this isn't as bad as it seems.

ANXIOUS ME: Exactly. It's probably much worse.

OPTIMISTIC ME: Well, no matter how this ends, I'm sure I'll come out of it an even stronger person!

Oh, by the way, I should have warned you, Optimistic Me uses exclamation points when trying to encourage positive thinking. Like a chipper fuckin' six-year-old in the Disney Store before she finds out she's only allowed to spend ten dollars, which will buy her exactly nothing. (Optimistic Me is so stupid.)

ANXIOUS ME: You just used the word "ends." How can you become a stronger person if you die? (Idiot.)

OPTIMISTIC ME: But I can be tough! I could totally beat cancer! Remember that time I scared those white-trash twins

---

[93] R.I.P., Bea Arthur. You are sorely missed.

who were bullying Glenn in middle school?! Taking on a couple of kids who were three inches taller than me took some bad-ass-ery.

It's true. Twin boys were bullying my little brother Glenn in sixth grade. They were mad because the girl they liked had a crush on Glenn. It was a love square. The twins told Glenn to meet them at Hicks's farm after school, presumably to kick his ass. (And yes, we lived behind a farm owned by people with the unintentionally un-ironic last name, Hicks.) I put on my shit-kicking boots (hiking boots, which, just that morning, I'd decided to call "the nutcrackers") and stomped like a boss to the designated show-down location. I was the middle child with two brothers, so I'd led a **thug life** (see "old ass"). Glenn trailed behind, regretting that he'd ever told me about the bullies.

I was livid, and I worked myself into a fury as we walked across the cow's field. (Wagner's "Ride of the Valkyries" from *Apocalypse Now* was playing in my head.) The twins were in the same grade as Glenn, but they were a few inches taller, and how *dare* they intimidate a smaller kid? Those two fuckers were lucky I didn't step in a cow paddy on the way. Hell hath no fury like a woman with shit on her shoe. It's the third leading cause of women committing violent acts, right behind being told "you can't do that because you're a girl" and hearing a male doctor say, "there are very few nerve endings in your cervix." #TrueStory

I had always been a good kid (I played clarinet in the marching band, fer fuck's sake!), but I imagined myself as a vigilante badass.[94] Taking the law into my own hands and kicking some twin ass would be all in a day's work for this endearing antihero. I had the strength of Jamie Sommers (*The Bionic Woman*), the moxie of Mary Richards (*The Mary Tyler Moore Show*), and more snark than Darlene Conners (*Roseanne*). The twins thought they were going to face a smaller, weaker opponent in my brother, so they were totally unprepared when his wild-eyed, crazy-haired, cussing, gangsta-bitch sista showed up. At this point, I was audibly humming the theme from *Rocky*. I think one of them peed a little. I threatened their little boy parts so loudly that a lady who lived and worked on the farm poked her head out of her trailer and told us to take our argument elsewhere. Which I did, because I respected my elders. (Unlike those two gangly, punkass kids who were not respecting my authority as a seventh grader.)

Finally, one of the twins got up the courage to push me (probably because I was right up in his grill and insulting his dangly bits), so I punched him in the face. That was the only time I ever hit anyone in the face (because I am a goddamned pacifist).

I immediately realized that I don't much care for punching faces, but as my dad used to say, "You won't know if you like something unless you try it."

Everyone should try punching a face once. There are plenty of

---

[94] I may have missed my calling as a superhero. All I'd have needed was a pair of knee-high boots and a cape. One time I threatened to turn a little boy into a little girl with one swift kick after I saw him abusing his dog. That kid was lucky I didn't have the ability to shoot lasers from my eyes, or I'd have given him a laser conization of his gonads.

assholes who have yet to be punched.[95] If you've never punched an asshole, we're going to need you to pick up the slack. If *you* are an asshole, go ahead and punch yourself in the face. (I'd punch myself, but I already reached my asshole-punching quota of one.) I won't suggest any names of particular assholes who deserve to be punched, because I'm sure you all know at least one *cough* Donald Trump *cough*. Go ahead and pop some orange racist motherfucker right on the kisser.[96]

After that day, the twins stopped bothering Glenn. (Or maybe they didn't and Glenn never told me, preferring an after-school beating to the humiliation of having his sister show up again ... not sure).

OPTIMISTIC ME: Hells yeah. I can be a badass sometimes! Those two punks couldn't bring me down, and neither can cancer!

ANXIOUS ME: You screamed curses at them and threatened to rip their balls off. They were scared because they were eleven. You were almost fourteen and furious, and with that out-of-control fucking hair of yours,[97] I'm sure they thought you were

---

[95] One early reader thought I was recommending to literally fist someone's asshole. How she went from punching to fisting is beyond me, but for the record, I am 100% against non-consensual fisting.

[96] This is just *really* bad advice. Don't punch anyone. Especially not Donald Trump. #ThrowGlitterNotPunches Punching people is almost as stupid as mentioning Donald Trump in your book right before he possibly becomes the new Supreme Leader of the United States and passes a law to behead anyone who implies that he's an orange racist motherfucker.

[97] Anxious Me can be very catty.

capable of carrying out the threat.[98] Besides, breast cancer doesn't respond to verbal threats, and even if it did, it doesn't have any testicles. (Moron.)

OPTIMISTIC ME: Well. I might as well quit obsessing. I probably don't even have cancer.

ANXIOUS ME: How the fuck do *you* know? You probably *do* have breast cancer. Shall we review your "high-risk factors" again? Not only does breast cancer run in your family, and not only are you a DES daughter ... but *your zodiac sign is a crab ... called Cancer!* (Dumbass.)

OPTIMISTIC ME: Alrighty, but do you know what legendary sea creature can kick a crab's ass? The Kraken. And you can't spell Kraken with K-a-r-e-n. So there you are ... even if I *do* have cancer, I'm going to crush it ... because my cancer-fighting powers are epic!!!!

ANXIOUS ME: Oh fuck me all to hell. Your only epic superpower is worrying. Cancer is going to **pwn** you (see "old ass"). You're in denial. (Nitwit.)

The spotlight fades and the curtain closes, as I lie on a sofa, drinking a martini with a pink bendy straw.

---

[98] If you ever come across an infuriated thirteen-year-old girl having a hysterical moment, be sure to avoid making eye contact. You don't want to be anywhere near the blast radius when that nuclear meltdown starts. And by thirteen-year-old girl, I mean me. At any age. Fran knows. (Just place the flowers and the handwritten apology on the floor and back away slowly.)

After long days of anxious waiting, I got the phone call from Dr. Cutter. I felt like one of those nervous fainting goats as I picked up the phone. (See drawing below.)

She gave me the bad news first. "We need to amputate your torso, immediately."

She quickly followed with the good news. "But don't worry. Two *Star Trek* nerds at MIT have invented a machine, upon which we can install your head. It has a red flashing light, so you'll be able to communicate by blinking once for yes and twice for no. It's actually pretty cool."[99]

Okay, that's not verbatim. Dr. Cutter said the results were "complicated." Like my medical records just got a Facebook update on their cancer-relationship status.

She said they found precancerous cells, called atypical ductile hyperplasia (ADH), which meant I had an increased risk of getting cancer. ADH is considered, by some, to be precancerous. The test also revealed cells called lobular carcinoma in situ (LCIS). Although carcinoma is part of the name, LCIS cells never become invasive cancer.

Oh, and thanks a lot, guys-who-name-cells (you wankers) ... way to scare the shit out of women.

Both ADH and LCIS are "cancer indicators," meaning they are often found in the company of cancer cells. The assholes of cells.[100] Nobody should hang out with cancer cells. They're the kind of "friends" who get you to do some ill-conceived stunt that leaves you badly injured just so they can post an "epic fail" video on YouTube.

The next step was to perform a larger biopsy, called a "wire localization breast biopsy," which would be done in the hospital. (Oh

---

[99] Only *Star Trek* fans will get this reference to Captain Pike from the original 1960s *Star Trek* TV Show, and hello, fellow *Star Trek* fans! This is the point in the book where we get to feel superior to the non-Trekkies who have no idea what we're talking about. We're so awesome. Live long and prosper. I'm doing the v-thing with my fingers. (And yes, I know not calling it the Vulcan salute makes me sound like I'm not a true *Star Trek* fan, but I am. I'm just not weird about it. I wrote about this on my blog, chroniclesofaboob.com.)

[100] Note: According to the Susan G. Komen website, there is recent evidence to suggest that LCIS is also a precancerous condition, meaning that LCIS *can* turn into invasive breast cancer. So, now I'm not sure if *anyone* is sure that LCIS is a pre-cancer or just a cancer indicator. Isn't this fun?

boy. Time for a prayer circle?) This procedure would start with a mammogram (Lawd, why do they always), where they would stick a wire into my breast (huzzah) as a guide to the location of the original core needle biopsy. This would tell the surgeon which area of my boob to excise. I would then be taken to the operating room, put into a "twilight sleep" (not as restful as it sounds), and my surgeon would perform the biopsy. I'd go home the same day with some codeine-type pain pills, while they sent the tissue sample off to a lab to check it for cancer (sounds super).

My take-away: "So you want to drill out even more of my boob because you think there might still be cancer in there, but this time you want to use a bigger drill." I may have said this in a high, trembling falsetto. (Dr. Cutter reluctantly conceded that this was *kind of* correct.)

I was going to say, "Why don't you marry my boob since you love it so much?!" But I didn't, because she was a humorless mutant.

This is when Optimistic Me threw in the towel. "Fuck. You were right, Anxious Me. I probably do have cancer. I can't beat cancer. I don't know what I was thinking."

Optimistic Me said something about needing to go outside to think, and I haven't heard from her since. Not even a **poke** (see "old ass") on Facebook. I should have known Optimistic Me would skedaddle. Nothing good ever comes from "having a think," in my experience. Thinking is the very last thing you want to do when you have anxiety, though it's impossible to stop.

I'm kind of glad Optimistic Me left, though. Optimistic Me wasn't helpful. She'd say bullshit like "chin up," "stay positive," and "try not to worry." Pfft ... good riddance, asshole.

So, you might be thinking, a wire localization biopsy? That doesn't sound too terrible. And you're right. It doesn't *sound* bad, and that was by design. On paper, it doesn't appear all that sinister.

No more than a yellow on the amber alert scale, but it's much worse than that. It's actually *very* alarming, because this type of biopsy is also called a … cue the Monty Python brass-band music before the "Spanish Inquisition" (bump bump baaaaa!) … LUMPECTOMY!

But wait … it's also known as a (cue the horns: bump bump baaaaa!) PARTIAL MASTECTOMY! Just shot right the fuck up to red alert, amirite?

I know! That was my first thought, too: I was like, whoa, slow your roll, Google … a partial what the fuck now? Hold the phone, you did *not* just call it a partial mastectomy? No fuckin' way. And Google was like: way. That's right, because it's called a partial mastectomy in certain social circles, like the *Yale School of Medicine*!

This is what the fucking Google machine does to me. Dammit, Google! Stop ruining everything! And by the way, guys-who-put-the-word-"carcinoma"-in-the-names-of-probably-benign-cells, you could learn a thing or two from the guys who named a partial mastectomy a "wire localization biopsy." Ever heard of obfuscation? You should try it some time. (Shitheads.)

Eeesh … see what happens when doctors start poking around in one's breast? They find shit. Shit the person attached to said breast maybe didn't really want to know about. Shit better left unfound, if you ask me. And I hear ya, all you people yammering about early detection. We get it! You're saving lives! But are you? Are you really? Ask Google if breast cancer is being over-treated.

So, my core needle biopsy wouldn't be the end of the excavation of my left boob. There was more digging to come. I just hoped that, when all was said and done, my boob didn't look like an abandoned quarry that needed a fence around it to keep teens from using it as a goddamned swimming hole in the summer. As you may have deduced, these procedures really scare the piss out of me. (If you haven't deduced this, did you skip ahead to this chapter?) The first biopsy was painful and nauseating enough, but this second biopsy had to be performed *at the hospital!* (Shit.)

Granted, I was happy I'd be knocked out for the partial boob removal part of the procedure, but I couldn't understand why I needed to be awake during the mammogram/wire insertion stage, unless they needed my assistance, and gawd help us all if they did. (Ask Fran how helpful I was when he needed me to hold still so he could remove a tiny splinter from my foot.)

I also learned that the radiologist would leave one end of the stiff guide-wire sticking out of my tit. Great. *So glad I'd be awake to see that.* Good God, had anyone thought this through? Honestly, if the precise placement of the wire was important (and I supposed it was, if they wanted to remove the correct part of my boob), wouldn't it be pretty risky to do it while I was conscious/trembling in fear? Call me silly, but I'm thinking the chances of me knocking that fucking wire out of position go way the hell down if I'm asleep ... no? The whole thing sounded very slapdash to me. (Turned out, they had a plan for protecting the exposed end of the wire. A very crappy plan.)

I was also nervous because my breast was still bruised and sore from the first biopsy. I could not *imagine* submitting it to another mammogram so soon, but my friend Steve told me she had her core needle biopsy in February, when they found stage 0 breast cancer (which is what I had). Then she had to wait four months for her lumpectomy—not by choice, but because she had no health insurance and needed to apply for a grant. (Don't get me started on the state of our health care system and how the World Health Organization ranks our country around 37th in the world, far behind most first-world countries with universal health care. Why did you even bring it up?) In June, when Steve finally had her lumpectomy, they found stage II breast cancer. So I figured I'd suck it up and schedule my lumpectomy sooner rather than later. Plus, I was looking forward to seeing the ass end of this anguish. All the waiting and worrying was wearing me the fuck out.

I suppose I should formally introduce you to my friend Steve. (I'm always kvetching with her about the state of my boob health.) Her name isn't really Steve. I'm just calling her that after the comedian Steven Wright, not only because she has the same dry, cynical, fabulous sense of humor, but also because in real life, they have the same initials, so it's like kismet. As a side note: I'm not going to call her Stevie, which I realize would be a better name for a girl, as in Stevie Nicks (and in fact, my friend looks a bit like Stevie Nicks), because it amuses me to talk about "my friend Steve's boobs."

Steve has got to be sick of hearing from me. Kudos to her for not rolling her eyes and telling me to call if I get an *actual* cancer diagnosis. After all she'd been through, Steve showed a great deal of restraint in not smacking me on the back of my head. Of course, she lives in New York and I live in Pennsylvania, which is pretty far to do any effective slapping.[101]

I was in a state, thinking I probably *had* cancer they just hadn't found yet. The lab already found ADH and LCIS cells in my boob, and depending on which study I read, that meant there was a 20–

---

[101] But wouldn't it be cool if you *could* slap someone from afar? There should be a service for this. Forget singing telegrams, I want to be able to send someone a slap-o-gram. I'd pay someone major coin to go knock on an asshole's door (of my choosing) and be like, "Hi, are you John?" Then, when John says yes, he gets a slap and a little handwritten card from me. And **ikr** (see "old ass")? I would spend sooo much money on this service. (The only downside is that I'd have to change my name and wear a hockey mask every time I answered my door.)

70% chance they *would* find cancer during the lumpectomy.[102] I'm not great at statistics, but I knew this meant I had a 99% chance of having cancer. (Anxiety helps me to over-think things through.)

Speaking of research studies, I'm finding it hard to make informed decisions regarding my breast health when there are so many conflicting studies out there. I need a fucking medical degree to figure out which study I should pay attention to, and who has that kind of time? Certainly not those of us who are dying of cancer.

Simply having ADH and LCIS means I have an elevated risk of getting breast cancer for the rest of my life. Which means I have to worry about this, like ... *forever.* Naturally, I hoped the lumpectomy wouldn't reveal any malignancy, but I was also mildly concerned (a.k.a. petrified) about my long-term prognosis. There was a good chance I'd end up in that unfortunate group of patients in the middle of a medical-treatment tug of war. On one end are the doctors who recommend aggressive preventative measures; on the other are those who question the benefits of these measures. Consequently, patients have to decide between the sucky option and the *uber*-sucky option. The preventative measures could be anything from taking estrogen-blocking drugs (which can cause other types of cancer— more on this later) to a prophylactic mastectomy! Oy, oy, oy! ... So, yeah ... happy thoughts, Karen! Happy fucking thoughts.

As I mentioned in Chapter 1, I called my dad to try to relay the news, then immediately started crying and hung up on him. It could not have been any more like the old joke about a Jewish telegram: "START WORRYING. DETAILS TO FOLLOW." I wasn't crying before I called him, but for some reason, relaying the information out loud broke me. Sorry, Dad.

---

[102] I know, I know ... I need to stop reading studies, but honestly, what the fuck is up with that spread?

I was more worried about additional surgery than I was about chemo (if it came to that). Surgery hurts, y'all! I was feeling irrationally over-confident that I could deal, just fine, with getting brutally sick in the comfort of my own home, but I wasn't as confident about dealing with **moar** (see "old ass") agonizing procedures. The core needle biopsy was bad enough. Plus, I hoped getting sick on chemo might help me fit into my skinny jeans. That's me. Always looking on the bright side.

I had Fran running interference with friends and family that week, as I wasn't feeling up to talking to anyone about the lab results or my prognosis. I just could. Not. Even. Yes, I was worrying obsessively. (It's a gift.) #HumbleBrag If I were a superhero, I'd be called either "Worry Woman" or "Anally Retentive Girl." (Unless "anally retentive" means "really good at sticking things up your butt," because if it does, then I'm definitely *not* that.)[103] For me, worrying is expecting doom at any minute and, when it doesn't come, expecting the level and severity of the doom to increase accordingly—like the way the lottery jackpot grows every week if no one wins.

Anyway, in an attempt to avoid having to update everyone individually, I added this to my Facebook status (see screen grab below):

---

[103] Or maybe I am and I could get rich smuggling drugs across the border. What? The exact same drugs we get here are so much cheaper in Canada.

It was Lola who had suggested building a meth empire, and I thought making tons of money before I died was a fantastic idea. I bet that's one of the biggest regrets dying people have: Not making enough money. That and wishing they'd spent a lot less time with their loved ones. #LifeHack But I was smart enough to know I'd need to avoid anything involving chemistry, so I started working on other get-rich-quick schemes.

This was in the middle of a really harsh winter. Our dogs had decided they didn't want to go outside again until spring, which was a major change in attitude for Fergus. We adopted him from a shelter, where he'd lived for most of his first seven months of life. He must have had very little time outside each day, because when we first got him, he lurved being outdoors so much that he didn't care if it was raining, sleeting, or hailing veterinarians. Even in the midst of a blizzard, he loved being outdoors. That changed after about a year. He turned into a little pansy who didn't want to get his dainty feet wet. No shit, he's a fuckin' poof now. Fran hates it when I call Fergus a poof ... but trust me, he's a poof.[104]

One day was an especially snowy and sleety mess. Our deck could have been used to host the Winter Olympics. It was an icy disaster. (Oh, and it turns out that FEMA[105] is surprisingly unhelpful in these situations.) I saw Maggie surreptitiously peeking into the dining room, obviously trying to decide if she could take a shit in there without getting caught (it wouldn't be the first time), but she didn't, because she's a good girl (and she saw me watching her). That's when I remembered that, about a year after we got her, I found a fossilized turd in our dining room that I SWEAR was from the previous Easter. And no, this is not a commentary on how infrequently I clean my house. Maggie was already a year old when we adopted her and she took a long time to house-train, and this leftover turd, in a little used room of the house, blended right in with the carpet. Her poo has chameleon-like powahz.

That's when the money-making idea hit me. It's like the best invention since the ShamWow. So, almost everyone's heard of Turkish carpets. Well, I was thinking there's an untapped market for a carpet that can actually *hide* pet turds, and I call it ... wait for it ... the TURDish carpet! I know! Why hasn't anyone already thought of this? I was asking myself the same thing. So simple, it's genius.

I was seeing a carpet empire in my future.

---

[104] I should add, Fran would still love and totally support Fergus' right to marry if it turned out he was a poof.

[105] Now I know what the "F" and "A" in FEMA stand for. It's Fucking Asshole. I can't believe I had to spell that out for you.

Then I figured, why not design some faux-urine stained area rugs? Just let that soak in for a second.[106] Maybe even some cat-vomit-patterned throws.

That led me to the idea of designing furry furniture, so your couch doesn't look like it has a few untidy pet hairs on it ... it looks *intentional!* I brainstormed the idea with Lola, who agreed there was a fortune to be made. (This is why we get along so well.) She even came up with a trade name: FURniture. I loved it, but suggested changing it to "Home FURnishings,"—to give us more flexibility. We settled on the slogan "Home FURnishings: Because nothing pulls a room together like pee stains and turds."

Unfortunately, Lola and I are procrastinators and we never followed through. Plus, neither of us wanted to make an appearance on HGTV. So, listen, if you want to take this idea and run with it, it's yours. Seriously, go forth and prosper, with our blessings.[107] I want readers to feel like they've gotten their money's worth from this book. Please put that in your Amazon reviews.

Anyhoozle, that was my big money-making scheme, and I was thinking about how the idea would kick some serious ass on *Shark Tank*, but then I remembered I wouldn't get to see it, because I'd be dead. My mind went back to obsessing about my looming lumpectomy. Knowing I had to go through another minor (major?) medical procedure, I was feeling very anti-social. I was tippy-toeing on a fine line between neurotic worry and full-blown panic.

---

[106] Please tell me you saw what I did there.

[107] Of course, if you wanted to give me a tip of the hat, you could manufacture a "Karen's Sofa Line," which would include fabric that has faux-wine stains and/or looks like spilled popcorn.

I stopped reading articles about breast cancer (I put away the Google). I didn't even want to hear any news about how early detection greatly increases cancer survival rates, because let's face it, there were no guarantees that I *had* caught it early, *or* that I had a type of breast cancer that responded well to treatment (fucking Google, for Christ's sake). There are incurable forms of aggressive breast cancer, and for all I knew, I had some new exotic cancer strain that kills within hours. Maybe modern science didn't even know about it yet, and they'd end up calling me "patient zero." Naturally, I'd be patient zero, 'cause I'm just that fantastically fuckin' lucky. I could imagine myself, as soon as my lumpectomy was over, being surrounded by doctors in hazmat suits, all wanting to see the woman with the most bizarre and deadly form of breast cancer ever known to man. They'd hover around me talking about how unbelievably quickly I was dying, and I'd start shouting, "I can hear you!"

Then they'd congratulate Dr. Cutter on her discovery. She'd probably want to name these new cancer cells after herself, calling them something like Cutter Malignant-ish Probablia Harmfulius cells (because she doesn't like to worry patients with scary terminology, like "partial mastectomy"). Sure, I'd argue that they should be called Karenicus Boobilla Carcinoma Fatalus, but I'd probably expire before I even got to the word carcinoma, because the name is so damned long and I only had seconds to live.

I was a nervous mess. Worse than a person with coulrophobia (the fear of clowns), sitting in the backseat of a Volkswagen Beetle, surrounded by a bunch of bozos in make-up, rainbow wigs, and big floppy shoes, heading to a clown party. In the weeks leading up to my lumpectomy, I performed more breast exams on myself than I had in my entire life. If I put a penny in a hat for each self-exam I'd done before I knew I needed a lumpectomy, then took one penny out for each exam I did while waiting for my lumpectomy, I'd have

... well, I'm not sure what I'd have, because I think it depends on the speed of the train and what time it left the station. #ShittyMath-WordProblems.

The results of my core needle biopsy were ambiguously worrisome, at best. At worst, they were an alarming portent of more frightening procedures and treatments to come. The brief phone call with my surgeon compelled me to ask Google, in a million different ways, "How quickly does a person who has ADH and LCIS die from breast cancer?"[108] Google can be more cryptic than a goddamned Magic 8 Ball. You have to keep rephrasing the question until you get the answer you want.

I tried to pass the time before my lumpectomy by coming up with other legacy-building, money-making ideas, but my heart wasn't in it. I maybe should have been drawing or painting, but I already knew I wouldn't live long enough to see my genius appreciated, which only pissed me off. (I'm sure the New York art scene is distraught/thrilled.) So yeah, instead of thinking positive thoughts and trying to implement the Law of Attraction, the only law I truly subscribed to was "Murphy's Law." I spent most of my days ruminating over what it would be like to die from cancer. Depressingly, it also became evident that I wouldn't live long enough to figure out how to properly end a chapter of a book. (I know, Lola, and I hate me for that too).

---

[108] Google never gave me a definitive answer and kept sending me to sites that had bullshit disclaimers like, "the advice contained herein should not be used as a substitute for a consultation with your doctor or other healthcare provider." Pffft ... I'll substitute it if I want. They're not the boss of me.

This chapter intentionally left blank

The lumpect-oh-my-god

ALLOW ME TO PROVIDE a brief recap of my boob story so far—to keep you all abreast, in a manner of speaking. I had a wonky mammogram in December (yippee), core needle biopsy in January (such fun[109]), and next, I had a lumpectomy scheduled (huzzah), where a good time would be had by all ... if "all" means the boobarazzi.

I spent most of the week leading up to the lumpectomy being *somewhat worried*. By the end of the week, I'd progressed to *moderately worried*. The day before my lumpectomy, I started out in a *considerably worried* state, quickly proceeded to *severely panicky,* and by late evening, I was in a crescendo of *near hysteria.*

Sleep was out of the question. Needing to get up at 5:30 a.m. made things worse. I usually get up at the crack of noon. Do you ever have that problem? You're acutely aware that you *need* to sleep, which only exacerbates the being-wide-awake problem. You try to

---

[109] And hello to you, my fellow Miranda Hart fans who recognized this phrase!

read, but can't concentrate. You put down the book and attempt to sleep, but you can't get comfortable. After tossing and turning, you give up and switch the light back on, which doesn't wake up your significant other, so you start poking him or her in the face, because you'd like someone to kvetch with. Right? We've all been there.

Just as I was getting ready to assault Fran's face with a pillow, he opened his eyes and asked "Why is the light on, and what are you doing with that pillow?"

ME: You can't sleep either?

FRAN: You just woke me up.

ME: Oh, did I wake you? Yeah? I was just lying here thinking about you, since after tomorrow I'll be dead and won't get to see you again ... but don't mind me ... you should get your rest.... You've got a busy few days coming up, what with planning the funeral and all. Go back to sleep.... I'll just go downstairs, watch some TV, and hope I don't watch a show with a cliffhanger that I'll never get to see.

FRAN: Okay.

He immediately fell back asleep. (Bastard.) His wife's approaching death was apparently no impediment to his ability to snooze. Of course, *I* wouldn't be able to get any sleep the night before *he* was going to die, but whatever. It's not like it's a competition over whose love is greater or anything. (But if it were, I'd win.)

So I went downstairs and watched the first season of *Will & Grace* for most of the night. Eventually, as often happens, the morning followed the night, and on that particular morning, I had to have a lumpectomy. Fucking mornings, amirite?

Oh! And what made the day just a skosh more perfect: I got my period that morning, complete with ~~tormenting~~ uncomfortable menstrual cramps. Super. I went code red *right* before surgery. Sorry, **TMI** (see "old ass"), I know, but my period is usually like clockwork, people. Fuckin' clockwork ... same exact time *every* month ... but since I was having surgery, Aunt Flo decided to visit early. I texted my friend Steve (see screenshot below):

I love love love her dry sense of humor.[110]

When I got to the hospital, I changed into a gown, and the nurse gave me some cheap, hospital-issued, one-size-fits-most, stretchy, white-mesh, disposable underwear and a maxi pad the size of a child's mattress (I'm bringing sexy back). After getting changed, I was led to a hospital stretcher in my own, reserved "parking spot" in the pre-surgery ward. The nurse closed the light blue drapes that serve as makeshift privacy walls, and I was careful not to eavesdrop on the conversation going on in the parking spot next to mine, because I respect other people's privacy.[111] Someone then led Fran into my "room," and a nurse came to give me an IV. When she was done, she left us to wait for the first procedure.

I highly recommend NOT getting any sleep the night before surgery. I had *maybe* slept for a very restless two hours on the couch, and that, combined with the Xanax I dry-swallowed before leaving the house, allowed me to doze off for about an hour in the hospital, which was truly *aaawwwwesommme!*[112] I wouldn't have believed it possible.

---

[110] Hey, old people, real quick: texting is sending someone a text message from your cell phone to theirs. Gr8 means "great" and "jit4" means "just in time for." As further clarification, the Muslim dictator from Kenya, with his Obamacare, causes wonky periods.</sarcasm> This is how Steve and I make fun of the Tea Party. Making fun of Tea Partiers makes everything better.

[111] It was an elderly couple, and their daughter Janet was going to come by the hospital later, after she dropped the kids off at school, but they weren't sure she would know where to go. Just as I was about to pull back the curtain and offer them my cell phone, I heard the man say he'd call her, so he must have brought his own.

[112] In my head, I said the word "awesome" here with a really high, sing-songy voice. Like on the do-re-me scale, it went from the "high do" (aaawww) to "la" (sommme). Now you do it. Do it!

An orderly woke me up when it was time for the first procedure. I was wheeled to the radiology department, where the ~~monster~~ radiologist stabbed me with a needle to place a wire in my breast *while giving me a mammogram* (whose fuckin' idea was that?) on my still very bruised and sore breast, where there was a barely healed incision from the core needle biopsy. This was the wire portion of the "wire localization breast biopsy," and it was massively unpleasant. Also, the radiologist gave me a shot of a local anesthetic, but didn't wait long enough for it to take effect.

It's possible that I inadvertently hurried the radiologist, Dr. Russian,[113] a bit. When he asked me how I was doing, I said I was scared. His response was, "Well, this won't take long."

He then rushed through the wire installation while my boob could still feel all the things. I should have tried to chat him up to give the anesthetic time to kick in, but neither of us spoke. I'll bet he didn't want to be stuck in the room with me any longer than he had to be. Fair enough. He probably sensed my NeedleMammoSlammo-Phobia (the fear of having a long needle stuck in your breast during a slammogram). The most common symptoms are shaking, jumping when touched, and the inability to engage in polite conversation. Also, because I was getting one step closer to the time of surgery, I'm sure I looked like I was about to start bawling like a tween girl who just found out Zayn left **One Direction** (see "old ass"). It's no wonder he was in a big fuckin' hurry to get me out of there.

My friend Steve told me later that she fainted during this part of her procedure and woke up on the floor with pillows under her head and feet. (I'm betting the mammogram machine, with its firm grip on her boob, prevented her from actually falling over. *That machine was pretty tight, y'all.* No doubt a nurse had to hold her up

---

[113] See what I did there?

before the radiologist could release her boob and lower her to the floor. Eeesh.)

Of course, there's a slim chance that the radiologist waited exactly the right amount of time for the numbing agent to work on me, and that I was simply exaggerating every minor sensation because I was hyper-aware of my already-tender and battered boob. I was tenser than a rat at a Jack Russell party. If the radiologist had so much as patted me lightly on the shoulder, I'd probably have shrieked, "Stranger Danger!" and immediately done an Irish goodbye (or a French exit, if you prefer).[114]

After the wire was in position, the doctor taped a paper cup over it to prevent the exposed end from getting bumped before surgery. This is the hospital's shitty solution to wire protection I mentioned earlier (see drawing below.)

---

[114] If you didn't already know, this is when you leave a party without saying goodbye. And now you can say you actually learned something while reading this book. Please add that to your Amazon review as well. Thanks in advance.

This happened,

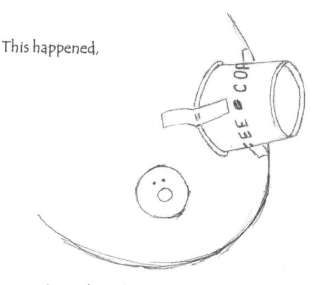

because hospitals suck at coming up with plans to
prevent perfectly placed boob wires from getting
knocked out of position.

Other than the fact that it was taped to my boob, it was a
wholly unremarkable paper cup. I showed it to Fran and told him to
start calling it "Exhibit A" (for my wrongful death suit). I couldn't
believe it. It stuck straight out of the side of my boob. I scared the
shit out of myself every time I accidentally jarred it with my upper
arm while trying to adjust my hospital sheets.

I still don't understand why they couldn't use something stur-
dier to protect this critically placed surgical guide. If it absolutely had
to be a DIY project, I'd have been happier with something more substantial—like a cabin made out of Lincoln logs, or a Lego structure
secured with extra-wide duct tape wrapped around my torso a dozen
times. Cheesus.

After the wire installation and paper cup application, I was
brought back to my parking spot in the pre-surgery ward to wait
again. My insomnia the night before paid off for a second time. If

not for my utter exhaustion, I would have spent that time falling to pieces, and Fran would have suffered some broken metacarpals, because crazy, frightened women sometimes have crazy strong grips. (It's a thing.) Instead, I think Fran got in a few rounds of Candy Crush Saga[115] on his phone, and I dosed fitfully. Other than the fact that I was half-naked, wearing a ginormous maxi pad, suffering with menstrual cramps, trying desperately to avoid freaking out about the metal wire sticking out of my boob, while lying on an uncomfortable hospital stretcher, it was the perfect time for a nap.

About an hour and a half (or a jiffy) later, I awoke to see Fran still sitting quietly next to me, and the orderly, who had arrived to wheel me to the operating room. The man who pushed my bed was a chatty sort, and he and Fran talked about the Philadelphia Eagles, which was totally inappropriate, since Fran should have been asking me who I wanted to leave my jewelry to or if I had any final words. I said goodbye (again) to Fran before the orderly wheeled me through double doors into a wide hallway, which led to about five operating rooms. Fran gave me a kiss and said, "Good luck, hon. I'll see you when you get out."

I said, "You always were an optimist. That's one of the things I loved about you. Take care of the dogs after I'm gone. By the way, I left you a note next to the fridge with instructions on how long to reheat all the sympathy casseroles you'll be getting over the next couple of weeks."[116]

I was left to wait alone on my hospital stretcher for another ten

---

[115] Have you played this game yet? How was life even possible before?

[116] Fran is forever asking about what microwave setting to use when reheating food. My answer is always the same: one minute on high, then check it. Still cold…? Stir and put it back in on high for another minute. I suspect he's hoping I'll reheat his dinner for him, but I always treat it like a serious question.

to fifteen hours (or forty-five minutes). To pass the time, I surreptitiously checked out a few of the other patients who were waiting to be wheeled into various operating theaters. We were like planes in formation, waiting to take off (or crash).

Directly across the hallway from me were various pieces of hospital equipment on carts. They looked abandoned, which was exactly how I felt. Every now and again, someone would come by and wheel a piece of equipment into an operating room. I waited impatiently for my turn. I hoped someone would eventually remember I was needed in the OR, though I was beginning to wonder if they'd started without me.

I wished Fran could have waited with me.

Nurses walked around, stopping to ask each patient what procedure they were having done. Yeah, they actually did that and … **WTF**? (See "old ass.") Don't *you* know what procedure I'm having? I could have kicked myself for not putting a Post-it note on my right boob that screamed in all caps, "NOT THIS ONE! THE ONE WITH THE WIRE STICKING OUT OF IT, YOU IDIOT!"

I needn't have been so worried,[117] as this was merely a part of their quality-control process and not a sign that they had no fucking clue why each patient was there. Like, I don't think I could have asked for a facelift or a boob job at the very last minute, though if liposuction had been on the menu, I might have considered it. The nurse asked the guy on the stretcher in front of mine which hip he was having replaced. For half a second (or more accurately, for the rest of the time I waited), I worried that the nurse would get our charts mixed up, and I'd come out of surgery with a titanium hip, and the older gentleman would have a piece of his left breast removed. And would my new titanium hip cause any problems with

---

[117] I just made myself **LOL** there (see "old ass").

my cancer radiation treatments? Would my hip start sparking like metal in a microwave? I was going to be really pissed if radiation would have cured me, but thanks to a new fuckin' titanium hip, there was nothing left to do but give me a mastectomy and chemo.

The anesthesiologist rudely interrupted these thoughts when he stopped by my stretcher to ask me questions, like, did I ever have any trouble breathing or swallowing? (*You mean, like, other than right now?*) Then he gave me some papers to sign[118] and told me he was going to give me "something to make me a little more relaxed" before I went into surgery. Pfft, do I *look* like I need drugs to relax me? (Okay. Probably.) But I said, "No thanks, pal ... I went to college. I've heard *that* line before."

All right, I didn't say that (and no, I wasn't Bill Cosby'd[119] in college ... calm down, Dad), but I *did* ask not to be given anything, as I wanted to be completely lucid when moving onto the operating table. I wanted to make sure my head and neck were in a comfortable position before they put me under. (I'd had my gallbladder removed years earlier, and I woke up with a sore neck. I didn't want to repeat that experience.)

The lumpectomy was, um, disquieting. I woke up three times during surgery. Yeah, *that* happened. Three (3) times. I was just as surprised as you are. And did I mention that I'd barely had any sleep the night before? How was that even possible? The first time I woke

---

[118] I may have agreed to donate my boobs, all my organs, my house, and my entire Super Ball collection to the hospital if I died on the table, which would suck, because my Super Ball collection is *really* good. I honestly have no idea what I signed.

[119] Bill Cosby drugged women (allegedly), then sexually assaulted them (allegedly), because apparently, he likes a side of rape with his Jell-O pudding (presumably).

up, I had an itch on my nose, but when I started to scratch it, someone grabbed my arm (or was my arm already strapped down?) and told me not to move. I had opened my eyes for just a moment and saw only a blue sheet—I guess one of those blue paper-drape thingies they use in operating rooms. Someone told me to relax and they knocked me out again.

The second time I woke up, I mumbled, "Can you please knock me out a little more?"

Call me un-neighborly, but I don't feel I should have needed to ask. I think I heard someone sort of apologize, and then they complied.

The third time I woke up, I remember being startled, and I jumped. It felt like someone had ripped tape off of my nipple (probably because someone *had* ripped tape off my nipple), and then I was aware of some fuss around me. I must have sat up a few inches, because I heard someone say, "Oh, sorry, Mrs. McCool. Lie back down, you're almost done now. We'll take you down to recovery in just a moment."

Recovery? I'm not sure I'm done with the not-supposed-to-be-awake part!

So, um, yeah ... "twilight sleep" my ass. More like "twilight conscious-enough-to-need-to-ask-to-be-knocked-the-fuck-out-again sleep." Cheesus. Wasn't the best day I'd ever had. Not the worst, either, though.[120] The good news: My stay in the recovery room was really short.

Chyaaaa! 'Cause I was half-awake for the whole fucking surgery!

---

[120] I once peed my pants in kindergarten. The school nurse tried to call my mom, who wasn't home, so one of our neighbors had to bring me a clean pair of pants and underwear. That sucked, and it was likely the reason why I have a pronounced fear of soiling myself.

The nurse in the recovery room looked surprised by how fully conscious I appeared just moments after they wheeled me in. She said, "Well, you sure look like you're already up and ready to go.... What can I get you to drink? We have grape juice, apple juice, orange juice ...."

I cut her off and said, "Vodka with a splash of cranberry."

She said, "Yep, you definitely sound like you're ready to go."

She also passed on a pro tip. She told me if I wanted to get out of the hospital quickly, I should tell the nurses in the next room that I want to go home, without waiting for them to ask, and she was right. It worked! I got out of the hospital very quickly after leaving the recovery room. Thanks, recovery room nurse!

I really shouldn't complain about waking up during surgery. Maybe I wasn't sedated enough because the anesthesiologist didn't take into account the size of my big fat ass when calculating the anesthesia dosage. A hospital gown can hide a lot. They're like muumuus. Also, I may have been off by five (or thirty) pounds when he asked me what I weighed, though I could tell he wasn't amused when he asked me to confirm my age, and I told him I was twenty-nine. (*I winked, dude! It was obviously a joke. No need to be a dick about it.*)

One other disturbing thing about the lumpectomy, though ... my surgeon used glue (spackle) instead of external stitches. Allegedly, the glue reduces scarring,[121] but my guess is that they use it because it takes less time to squeeze out some glue than it does to stitch someone up. A friend of mine, Cindy (her real name ... I hope she doesn't mind), is the one who pointed out that it sounded like they

---

[121] Pfft ... false-advertise much? A year later, I still had a very large, pronounced, pink scar. I should report that skin-glue company to the Better Business Bureau.

were doing a craft project on my boob, and she was right. The only things missing were rainbow glitter and googly eyes. (Wouldn't that have been fun if they'd stuck googly eyes on my boob? They should start doing that.)

The "skin glue" was clear, and it wasn't covered with gauze or tape or anything, which basically meant that I could see my Frankenboob with the full, foot-long (three-inch) laceration (incision) in all its lovely, bluish-red, swollen, horrifying-ness. The surgeon didn't even bother to remove the drawing she made in purple pen before the surgery, which included an outline around half my areola. Holy what the fuck?! Was my nipple under direct threat? In order to avoid cutting into it, she drew a purple half-circle around it? As if a purple pen mark would be the last stronghold before she slipped the scalpel right the fuck into my nipple? Yikes!

Thanks for the purple pen mark, but really? I'd have preferred something a bit more substantial to prevent an accidental nipple slicing ... like maybe tape a coffee cup over *that* area as well ... not only to act as a strong visual cue, but also as a physical barrier to ensure that she "cut no friggin' further!" Is that too much to ask? The hospital already had the paper cups!

Sisters, can I get an amen?

I guess I should be happy she didn't use bubble gum to seal my incision, but still, I don't feel that the wire or my nipple had the kind of protection they deserved. And don't get me started on my theories about why taping a paper cup to a boob counts as surgical prep.[122] But come on, if we're really doing this, why not tape a cup over the areola to keep it out of danger, too? Anyone?

---

[122] My theory is that Starbucks decided to expand into medical equipment, in case the five-dollar-cup-of-coffee industry ever takes a shit. That way, they can stay relevant with the **hipster** (see "old ass") population as they age.

Seriously ... why?

If I had known my nipple was going to be in jeopardy, I would have grabbed one of those pointy paper cones from the water cooler and taped it on myself, à la Madonna, circa 1990. And I would have painted it bright orange, like a fuckin' traffic cone. Do I need to think of everything?

Oy ... and by the way, that "pre-planning," purple-line sketch the surgeon drew to indicate where she would make the incision on my boob was *totally* ignored. She completely missed the purple line with the scalpel. I don't know what the fuck happened there, and okay, it wasn't like she was a mile off, but shouldn't surgery be more of an *exact* science? At least make an *attempt* to cut on the line. Good Lord. And if the purple pen was used to mark where she planned *to cut* with her scalpel, why did she use the *same* pen to mark the border of my areola? What exactly was the plan there? Cheesus!

And I get it, hospital cutbacks, rationing, they couldn't afford a second paper cup, whatever ... but at the very least, use a different colored pen! Like a spray-on, neon-pink paint for the area you do NOT want to cut? Am I wrong? Purple means cut ... hot pink means CAUTION!

This should be basic quality control. I told Lola about the taped paper cup, and she asked if I was at a real hospital or if Fran had dropped me off at a 7-Eleven and told them I was there for surgery.[123] Lola then strongly advised me *not* to have a lumpectomy performed at a 7-Eleven. She told me this *after* I had surgery. Thanks for the heads-up, Lola. Sheesh.

Side note: I did check for scars around my kidneys and, unless

---

[123] In case you don't have 7-Elevens where you live, they're a chain of quick-stop markets where, among other things, you can buy different sausage-shaped "meats" that have been rotating on a hotdog grill since legwarmers with matching headbands were a thing.

they removed one laparoscopically through the large gash in my boob, I'm pretty sure I still have them both. Phew. Thanks again to Lola, for suggesting I double-check.

Anyhoo, the surgery went fine. I was shaken up, but otherwise okay.

When I got home, I looked at my boob in the mirror and thought I should take a picture of it (with my nipple covered for modesty, of course); otherwise, nobody was going to believe just how far off my doctor's cut was from the purple incision line. Would it be such a bad idea to document it for proof, in case someone said, "Pics or it didn't happen'" (internet friends can be so skeptical)?

I made Fran monitor the titty wound every hour, because the bruising kept getting worse, and I wanted to make sure he saw it at its very peak of badness, before it started to fade. Best that he knew just how painful it was so he would keep asking if there was anything he could get for me.

After Fran went to bed, I started thinking I should definitely take a picture of my boob to show him in the morning. Then I recognized what a really stupid idea it was to take boob pictures the night of the surgery, while I was still under the influence of anesthesia and painkillers. Mercifully, I didn't make that boneheaded mistake.[124]

Day two: I couldn't believe how bad my boob got overnight. It looked like someone had taken a knife and carved out a big chunk (... oh, wait). So yeah, I have a few pictures of my Frankenboob on my laptop now. What? I was still on narcotics. And no, I did *not* post any pics on Facebook! I'm not that stupid.[125] But don't ask to see the photos, because nobody is *ever* going to see them. (Unless you get

---

[124] I took pictures the next day when the light was better.

[125] The scar made me look fat.

me really drunk and catch me off guard.)

Please don't try to get me really drunk and catch me off guard. I already know *exactly* which of my friends will attempt to do this, and I plan never to drink around any of them, ever again.[126]

I should add that this chapter was very sarcastic and negative. The hospital where I had my procedure is part of a network of hospitals that is ranked among the top in the nation (by *U.S. News & World Report*), and my surgeon was wonderful. She was very patient in answering all of my questions and giving me information (both the good and the bad), so I really did (and do) feel as though I was in excellent hands, even though she didn't have a sense of humor. Everyone who took care of me at the hospital was extremely kind and caring. But I really did wake up three times during surgery ... not even lyin'.

I'd have only one suggestion for my hospital's customer service comment card: "I'm deducting one star from your review because your recovery room appears to have run out of vodka. Not cool."

So, with much relief, this long-anticipated/dreaded surgery was over, and I was able get back to feeling only *somewhat worried* as I waited for the results of the biopsy/partial amputation.

---

[126] Or until the weekend.

Chapter 10

Lumpectomy results: Hoo-fuckin'-ray

WHILE WAITING FOR THE lumpectomy results, I kept myself busy by deciding who should inherit my various personal items. I got some stickers and started putting price tags on the stuff to be sold at my upcoming, pre-death estate sale. Fran said there's no such thing as a "pre-death estate sale." He kept insisting it's called a "garage sale" (you say potato), so I put a sticker on his truck, leaving it to my nephew Kyle, since his sister Chiara was getting my car. I never got around to having my estate sale though, because I got bogged down trying to pick out my cremation urn. (So many choices!)

Finally, Dr. Cutter called with my lab results, which were good(ish). No malignancy was found ... yet. They found more of the same types of pre-cancerous/abnormal cells they saw in the previous biopsy. You may be thinking I sound particularly pessimistic for someone who didn't have breast cancer, but even Dr. Cutter, as she was relaying this seemingly good news, reiterated that I am still at an elevated risk of getting breast cancer in the future and would need to be monitored closely. It was like winning a pick-three scratch ticket, if winning a pick-three scratch ticket meant the weekly payout was to worry about breast cancer for the rest of your life, in lieu of a lump sum in cash (better luck in your next incarnation).

Dr. Cutter wanted me to speak with an oncologist to discuss options for "mitigating" my risk.

The other slightly disappointing news was that I wouldn't get to lose any weight on the chemo diet. #DashedHopes.

After I got the news that I didn't have cancer, which Fran and my parents were thrilled about, I couldn't help but feel like the worst wasn't over—as if this were only a brief reprieve. Also, my anxiety never subsides immediately. I felt as though it was only a matter of time before the other shoe dropped. The shoe with all the boob cancer in it. Maybe this is what combat veterans with PTSD feel like. Scarred physically and expecting another battle at any moment.

Dr. Cutter wasn't especially congratulatory. There was no glass of champagne or a cupcake waiting for me at my surgical follow-up a week later, though I feel like this should be standard medical practice. What? It's not like I'm asking for a fuckin' parade. (But honestly, if a bunch of drunken Irishmen can manage to organize one every March, it can't be all that difficult.)[127] I think, if a biopsy comes back benign, or even benign-ish, like mine, *someone* at the doctor's office should organize a party to help the patient with transitioning back to normal life.

Wait. Come to think of it, I have this backwards. If you *are* diagnosed with cancer, the doctor should say, "I'm terribly sorry, Mrs. McCool, your condition is terminal. Would you like a cookie and this bottle of Jägermeister?" (Yes, please.)

---

[127] Was that racist? Please don't put the part about me being racist in your Amazon review. **TIA** (see "old ass").

Dr. Cutter told me about some options to discuss with my on-cologist, including taking an estrogen-blocking drug. She said this drug, Tamoxifen, reduces the risk of getting breast cancer in women who have an elevated risk. Pfft ... like I'm stupid. If the drug helps women with an elevated risk, why wouldn't it help ALL women? Why isn't everyone taking it if it's so fucking magical, hmmmm? I knew there had to be some kind of catch. And I was right (more on this later).

Dr. Cutter also briefly mentioned a prophylactic mastectomy (yikes!), but after seeing my face, she quickly added that it wasn't the first thing on her risk-mitigation to-do list.[128] Additionally, she wanted me to see a genetics counselor. There is something called Lynch syndrome, which is a hereditary disorder that has shown some relationship between breast cancer and colon cancer. Since one of my maternal aunts had colon cancer and another maternal aunt had breast cancer, Dr. Cutter thought it prudent for me to be tested for this syndrome. She also wanted me to have the test for the BRCA gene mutation, which is disproportionately found in those of Ash-kenazi Jewish heritage. (I can't believe how shitty cancer treats Jewish women.) I was feeling really good about the second test, though, be-cause I studied really hard. PA HA HA HA ... ha ha ... ha ... hehe ... hmmm. (Yeah, she didn't laugh at that either.)

I keed. I was confident I didn't have this gene, since my dad's sisters had already tested negative and, on my mom's side, only one sister in four had contracted breast cancer. I'd have to have incredibly shitty luck if I managed to escape inheriting the BRCA gene from my Ashkenazi Jewish grandmother and, instead, inexplicably got it from my mom's Scottish, Protestant side of the family, right? Cue

---

[128] I suspect the face I made was somewhere between "oh no!" and "I will cut you, bitch."

the announcer voice-over: "This sick cosmic joke is brought to you by The Irony Bus. The Irony Bus, your one-way ticket to YouJust-GotFuckedVille."

So, even though I got good news (no malignancy), I wasn't feeling especially celebratory, and I didn't want to talk to any friends or family about it. I wasn't nearly as relieved as you'd think I'd have been. I thought about sending an email that said, "It's not cancer ... woot! ... But please don't call or email to high-five me right now ... **kthxbai**." (See "old ass.")

I still felt like I was destined to die of cancer one day and needed to prepare myself not to wig-out when that day came. I had two narrow escapes already (cervical and breast) ... well, okay ... maybe "narrow" is a bit extreme ... but I'm pretty fuckin' confident my obituary isn't going to say "she died peacefully in her sleep."

And I get it, we're all going to die. Life's a terminal disease, after all, so I need to stop being so worried about medical procedures (as sucky as they are), and I especially need to stop obsessing about what my "end of life" might look like. I just wish my eventual death would come in the form of a fast, fatal heart attack. (And yeah, preferably in my sleep, if anyone who grants wishes is listening. I'm looking at *you*, God.) That sounds so much less stressful. Being hit by a bus would be awesome, too, but I'd have to drive into town, and finding a parking spot is *such* a pain in the ass.

I'm not saying I wanted to die right away. I just wanted it to be quick when the time came.

Fran, however, was absurdly pleased when he heard the news.

FRAN: Oh, thank God. What a relief.

ME: What's to be so relieved about?

FRAN: That you don't have cancer!

ME: But I may still get breast cancer in the future. I'm officially at a very high risk.

FRAN: Yes, but you also may *never* get cancer, and we know for sure, *you don't have it right now.* That's awesome.

ME: I don't follow you.

All I knew was that my lady-parts had tried to kill me twice already, and I didn't think they had any intention of stopping. Eventually, I was gonna get wacked.

Chapter 11

Oncology offices may cause diabetes and a brief word about tamoxifen

I F YOU LIKE CANDY, you should totally visit an oncology wait-ing room. There were so many candy dishes around my oncologist's office that I half-expected a little orange man with green hair to escort me to the exam room via a gondola on a chocolate river. That's how much candy they had. It was spooky.[129]

I grabbed a seat and looked around the reception area, which had a kind of upscale decor—a combination of muted lime-green and chocolate-colored prints, with just a hint of diabetes. Most of the employees had muted lime-green personalities, as well. They were all pleasant enough, in an emotionally distant kind of way. Hu-

---

[129] *Willy Wonka & the Chocolate Factory* was a straight-up horror movie for kids. Remember when that fat kid fell in the chocolate river and got sucked into the pipes? And those freaky Oompa Loompas? In a word, unnerving. And don't even get me started on the "child catcher" in *Chitty Chitty Bang Bang*.

man resources probably weeds out all the excessively cheery receptionists so oncology patients don't reach over the counter and punch them in the throat. I read a poll once that said almost 80% of doctors support the use of medical marijuana. I don't know if it would cure anything, but it certainly would improve the vibe in their waiting rooms.

Everyone behind the desk looked a bit tense, which made me wonder if they were back there drawing straws to determine who was going to have to tell me how long I had to live.

At first, the candy dishes distracted me from my worries, like a fish with a shiny object (as intended, no doubt). The dishes practically screamed, "Everything will be fine. Look! Bonbons!"

This didn't fool me for long, though. I was still preoccupied with dying of cancer. In fact, I was sure I'd read somewhere that there was a study linking excess sugar consumption to cancer. Not that I'm impugning any motives, of course (but it couldn't hurt their job security, right?). And did someone just call an Irony Taxi? 'Cause it looks like it's about to make a pickup when all these patients die from the diabetes they got at the oncology office.[130]

I selected a peppermint candy (see drawing below). I love these because a) they're just like candy canes only without the cumbersome hook part; b) they're delicious; and c) they make my breath minty fresh. It's not just a candy, it's a socially awkward–situation saver.

---

[130] My apologies. That wasn't funny. Because cancer patients dying from diabetes isn't humorous, but mostly because I already used an irony bus joke in the last chapter.

Suck it, butterscotch.

Do oncology offices have a lot of experience with dying people and stinky breath? Probably. As I was sucking on my candy, I began to wonder who I'd have to waterboard to find out how long I had to live. I unwrapped another peppermint and, uncharacteristically, I found myself starting to enjoy the waiting room. Damn these people and their soothing mints! Just as I was getting lost in these thoughts, my name was called. A nurse was already escorting me back to see the oncologist. I hadn't even been there ten minutes. It's like the closer to death you are, the faster they get you in. And note to self: Don't shove any more peppermint candy wheels in your mouth than you can comfortably fit in your cheeks. Some nurses like to chit chat. #ImmediateRegrets.

Let's call my oncologist Dr. Tumorstein. She looked like she'd just had her bat mitzvah ten days earlier. She may have been around my age, but she looked younger. (Well, I'd look younger, too, if I'd never had a cancer scare. My hair started to turn gray when I was twenty-six. Not that long after my cervical cancer scare. Coincidence? I think not.)

Dr. Tumorstein was amicable, but I think she assumed I had no idea why I was there. I say this because her first question was, "Do you know why you're here?"

It's possible she thought I was clueless in general. I often exude the vibe of a disheveled idiot. As I already touched on, my fashion sense is a cross between "ten-year-old kid" and "homeless person." (In my defense, it takes a surprising amount of effort not to give a fuck about your attire.) I try to dress like someone who spends her days in a lounge chair, reading *MAD Magazine.* (Because dress for the job you want.) I mostly wear jeans, a t-shirt, and old sneakers. When I feel like getting dolled up, I throw on a button-down Hawaiian shirt. (They're dressy 'cause they have buttons.) I first started wearing these shirts in high school, when a local radio station did a weekly shtick called "Hawaiian Shirt Gonzo Fridays."[131] The goal was to get everyone to wear Hawaiian shirts to ring in each weekend, because that's how you effect meaningful change in the world. My friends and I would wear Hawaiian shirts on Friday nights, because a) we were trend setters; b) we thought they made us look cool and quirky (no doubt we actually looked like ridiculously enthusiastic tourists at a super shitty luau); and c) we considered the shirts to be a sign that we were refined listeners of a classic rock station, as opposed to lame fans of crappy bubble-gum pop radio.

Dr. Tumorstein looked stylish and exuded confidence. (She probably never wore Hawaiian shirts). Great, so on top of feeling nervous, I felt, by comparison, like a disheveled moron. When she asked me if I knew why I was there, her tone reminded me of the way a compassionate nurse might ask a confused homeless person if they knew why they were in the psych ward. I was careful not to give an answer that made me sound like an imbecile (even though I was dressed like one). I moved the last peppermint wheel into my right

---

[131] Shout out to anyone who grew up in the Philadelphia, PA area and remembers what I'm talking about! Good times, amirite?

cheek and started to pontificate. I threw in a lot of medical terminology so she could tell I was a college graduater.

I said,

"Well, I recently had a core needle biopsy followed by a wire localization breast biopsy in which the pathology lab found ADH cells ... errr... you know ... atypical ductile hyperplasia ..."

I paused and looked at her to make sure she was duly impressed that I knew what the acronym meant. She was.

"... as well as *LCIS, or lobular carcinoma in situ*, which, even though it has the word 'carcinoma' in it, isn't really cancer."

I used air quotes when I said the word "carcinoma," so we could both mock the guys who name cells. This would be our first inside joke, as friends.

"... but boy, that scared the shit out of me before I found out *'in situ'* means 'in place,' which means *not malignant ...* "

I waved my right hand dismissively to show how I wasn't concerned about LCIS anymore, even though I was, because I didn't want her to think I was going to be one of those super needy friends. I continued:

"... but from what my breast surgeon told me*, these two types of cells are cancer indicators*, and did I tell you? I had *pre-cancerous cells on my cervix once*, and had to have a *laser conization,* which wasn't fun. But I made the surgeon, who was a really pompous man, knock me out, even though he didn't want to ..."

We were bonding over being independent, powerful women in a man's world. It can be hard, but now we knew we'd have each other's backs. We were like Thelma and Louise, only without the flying car.

> "... and oh, before I forget, the cervix thing was probably due to my mother having taken *DES* when she was pregnant with me (it's probably in my file), and I know, right? I'm like waaay too young to be a *DES daughter* ... all my doctors have mentioned it."

I snuck a look at her to see if she thought so, too (she nodded). That's the kind of friends we would be. We'd compliment each other all. the. time. You'd barely have to drop the hook in to start fishing for one before there was a compliment tug on your line. We'd also constantly do little things for each other, but I figured it would be weird to ask her to braid my hair right then.[132]

> "... but I don't blame my mom, because she was only trying to have a healthy baby, and it was obviously her doctor who was the total asshole. Funny story ... his wife later killed him with a pillow (allegedly). You should look him up."

I think she was intrigued, but you know how I hate to digress, so I didn't go into the story. Plus, it would give us something to talk about when we had coffee later. I continued,

> "... so, anyhoo, my breast surgeon told me the *cells in my breast are cancer indicators*, which, as you know, means that along

---

[132] Not because it was too early in our relationship (is it ever too soon to start braiding each other's hair?), but because the exam table was too small for us both to sit cross-legged.

with my *DES exposure, I'm at a higher risk for getting breast canc...*"

She stopped me there and jokingly said, "Sorry, that wasn't meant to be a quiz."[133]

Uh-oh. Maybe Dr. Tumorstein was starting to suspect that her first impression was right, and that I *was* a scared imbecile. Was she laughing with me, or at me? She had a relaxed manner that (eventually) put me at ease, and I liked her, but if she was going to be one of those "story interrupters" who likes to butt in so they can tell you about their own, much better story, she was never going to earn that half a heart from our "best friends" necklace. Nobody likes an interrupter, let alone a one-upper. Cheesus. I wondered if maybe I should leave her a copy of that article "Five Tips to Help Your Relationship Flourish" on the exam table when I left.[134] That, or I'd have to start coming up with reasons why I never called her back, or why I didn't go to her stupid dinner party, and then my next oncology visit would be super awkward.

I figured I should stop her and say, "Just so you know, I'm not really looking for any new friends right now. It's totally me, it's not you."

But I didn't, *because I don't interrupt people.* So I told her with my eyes. She looked back at me, clearly ~~puzzled~~ hurt. But it would have hurt a lot worse if I'd waited to break it off until after I'd finished weaving our lime-green and chocolate-colored matchy-matchy friendship bracelets.

---

[133] It may be worth noting that I forgot to take Xanax before this appointment.

[134] Maybe I'd also circle and highlight step four, which says, "Avoid Being Passive Aggressive." That one's important.

We discussed my biopsy results, and she suggested I have a breast MRI in a few months, followed by a mammogram six months after that. We also talked about the new "3D mammogram" machines. This digital technology increases cancer detection significantly over standard mammograms. I asked Dr. Tumorstein if they could also add some digital effects to make my breasts look perky again, so I could sext them to my husband. She chuckled at that, so at least she had a sense of humor. Still, she was smart, cute, and skinny, so I totally did the right thing when I broke up with her. Who needs friends who are better looking than you? Amirite? Might as well wear an invisibility cloak.

She suggested I get into a routine of alternating between mammograms and MRIs, so machines would be touching my boobs every six months. I agreed, though I wasn't sure I could do an MRI. I had a panic attack while getting an MRI on my neck. I had no idea how claustrophobic I was until that day. I lasted about 30 seconds in the MRI tube (no shit—not even a minute) before I started pressing the little panic button they gave me to hold.

The oncologist told me breast tissue changes as we get older, and that I had "fibrocystic breasts," which means my breasts are fairly "dense." Denser breasts make it harder for mammograms to detect any problems. (I didn't think my breasts were *that* stupid, but I guess I'm biased. Hey-oh!)[135]

---

[135] When I told Lola about this she said, "Sorry about your dumb breasts, Karen. Have you tried playing Mozart for them? It works for fetuses. (Just a suggestion ... geez)." Lola and I also learned we'd both had our gallbladders removed. Lola said, "You don't have a gallbladder? I don't have a gallbladder! We should have a club. If we get enough people, we can form a militia and declare war on all the people who have gallbladders. (I find them snooty.)" I mention this because, if you, dear reader, don't have your gallbladder, you should contact us. Our evil militia needs more gall-less militians. (Also, we may not know how to properly militia.)

Dr. Tumorstein also said breast tissue gets fattier as we age. I said, "I'm pretty sure that's already happened to my ass." She laughed and took a second to get herself together. (So this is how she treats a friend after an amicable split? She laughs at her fat ass? That's a tad frosty. It's not like I borrowed some of her clothes and never returned them, though if she ever loaned me that scarf she was wearing, she definitely wasn't getting it back now. And yeah, she wore a silk scarf. Never in my life have I ever worn an outfit-matching scarf for the sake of fashion. Is it any wonder I was starting to dislike her?)

She told me I was a good candidate for a drug called tamoxifen, which, as I mentioned earlier, is an estrogen blocker. (Certain types of breast cancer lurv estrogen.) I had looked this up when my breast surgeon mentioned it, and I read that tamoxifen has some very scary, *major*, though rare (*allegedly*), side effects including uterine cancer and blood clots leading to a heart attack/stroke. Yikes.

So now I'm thinking, okay doc, this is where you and I definitely part ways. (This was starting to feel like the worst cancer intervention, ever.) I asked her, "Yeah, but how would we even catch uterine cancer? I do breast self-exams (sometimes, when I'm really bored), but I don't think there's an equivalent self-exam for the uterus, right? Is there such a thing as an uter-ammogram?"

Dr. Tumorstein mumbled something about getting yearly pelvic exams by my gynecologist, but she didn't sound super confident in her explanation. The whole thing sounded bad to me. My anxiety alarms were going off. Wouldn't a tumor have to be pretty fuckin' huge to be felt during a pelvic exam? (I found out a little over a year later: The answer is yes. Yes, the tumor will already be huge.)

Dr. Tumorstein could tell I was feeling uncomfortable and told me the choice was mine. Tamoxifen was just one option and something to think about. In addition to the rare side effects, I told her I didn't like the sound of the more common ones, either, like meno-pausal symptoms, nausea, vaginal dryness (ummm, dry what now?), fatigue, and weight gain. Great ... weight gain ... I needed to gain more weight like I needed a hole in my boob. Errr ... wait.... You know what I mean.

Of course, it would be nice to have an *excuse* for being fat. If anyone noticed I'd gained weight, I could always shout, "I'M ON DRUGS TO PREVENT CANCER, ASSHOLE! AND THE DRUGS MAKE ME GAIN WEIGHT! SO FUCK YOU IF I'D RATHER BE FAT THAN DIE OF CANCER!" I could even put that on a t-shirt.

Ultimately, I decided to hold off on taking tamoxifen. Taking a drug that can cause something worse than it's supposed to prevent didn't sound like a great plan. Did I mention I'm a DES-daughter? Yeah. Fool me once, pharmaceuticals.

A brief word about tamoxifen

So now, both my surgeon *and* my oncologist were gently nudg-ing me toward tamoxifen, and no one likes a **noodge** (see "old ass"). The cell types in my biopsy meant I had a 30–40% chance of getting cancer within the next ten to twenty years, as opposed to most women, who have a 10–13%. (At least I think that's what the oncol-ogist said—my internal scare-o-meter tends to tune out all external input after the c-word, but I'm pretty sure the surgeon told me the same thing.) Tamoxifen would have (allegedly) cut my chances in half, or back to an almost average level of risk. There is, however, some controversy over using tamoxifen as a cancer preventative in patients who never actually had cancer. Tamoxifen is widely ac-cepted to be of benefit for patients who did have cancer (especially if the cancer has spread to a lymph node), and it helps to prevent the further growth of any cancer that chemo may have missed, but it's not all that beneficial for those who never had cancer.

My friend Steve started taking tamoxifen after chemo and, for her, the side effects were worse than the chemo. She said, "For me, tamoxifen was the worst. For some people, it is very difficult. I was one of those people. I cannot even ... man, it was awful. For some people, it is fine."

Steve was switched to another drug called Femara, which also has some terrible side effects (if you consider "making your whole body hurt" to be terrible. And I do!), but she said it was much better than tamoxifen. I realize, of course, many women tolerate tamoxifen very well, but again, it's the scarier side effects that I'd like to avoid, especially since the benefits for someone like me are still questionable.

Steve sent me this link to an article on Breast Cancer Action's website about tamoxifen:

http://archive.bcaction.org/index.php?page=newsletter-35a

The article is critical of the tamoxifen studies and of its use as a cancer preventative. You can also google the words "tamoxifen," "controversial," and "prevention," and you'll find lots of articles. Since everything on the internet is true, you can believe all of it. Happy researching. (Don't you hate it?)

One of my paternal aunts who hadn't had breast cancer was in one of these studies. She qualified because her mother and two sisters had breast cancer. If you ask me, "study" is an apt name for what these researchers were doing. Have they ever heard of the "observer effect," from physics, where the act of observation changes the thing being observed? What if, in these studies, the thing being observed (the patient) changed in a really bad way (got uterine cancer)? Eeek. Isn't that like using a magnifying glass to "study" the effects of sunlight on ants.

I also bought a book called *Tamoxifen and Breast Cancer*, by Michael W. DeGregorio and Valerie J. Wiebe. I have no plans to read it myself (you know my position on "the more you know"), but it's in my library in case anyone asks why I'm not following my doctor's recommendations. I can throw this book at them and yell, "BECAUSE THIS!"

I don't think it makes me completely insane to think a chemical/pharmaceutical solution might not be the best plan of action.[136] I'm not convinced that taking a drug that can cause uterine cancer to only "somewhat" or "maybe" lower my risk of breast cancer is a good trade-off. I subscribe to the "first, do no harm" approach. How much harm can there be in avoiding a drug that may cause more harm?

Of course, doing nothing isn't always the best choice, either. For example, if you find yourself hurdling down a hill on a sled heading straight for a tree, you may not want to do *nothing*. You may want to try to possibly do *something*, like, say, try to avoid hitting the tree (take tamoxifen)—except that maybe, in avoiding the tree (breast cancer), you hit a big rock (uterine cancer), instead. You might even bounce off the rock and hit the tree, anyway. That would totally suck.

I was hoping my sled would narrowly miss the tree, and I decided not to do anything that could increase my rock-hitting chances. Was that wishful thinking? Maybe. Statistics should probably have been considered. Maybe I should have weighed my tree-hitting chances against my rock-hitting chances, but there were so many conflicting statistics from multiple studies, how was I supposed to decide which studies to pay attention to? It's like what Lola once told

---

[136] What makes me completely insane is my fear of shitting in public toilets.

me about eggs:

> Is the whole modern-medicine thing one giant, ridiculous scam, or what? It's like eggs. "They're good!" "No, wait! They're bad! Stay the fuck away from eggs! Eggs kill!" "Whoops, we were wrong, lol! Eggs are good again! Eat all the eggs! But whatever you do, don't drink coffee!"

Go home, modern medicine. You're drunk.

The worst part is that I'll have no one to blame but myself if the shit hits the breast cancer fan, and without being able to shake my fists in the air in outrage at some stupid fuckin' doctor who screwed me over by not insisting on tamoxifen, what have I got left? Regrets, probably.

It was scary, no matter what. Take the drug and worry about having a stroke or uterine cancer. Don't take the drug and worry about getting breast cancer. It was like a win-win, only without any win.

I decided semi-annual 3D mammograms and MRIs would have to be enough, as I wait for my lady-parts to make their next move.

Nudging me to go on tamoxifen notwithstanding, I felt like I was in good hands with my oncologist (even though our being besties hadn't worked out). She was incredibly warm and genuinely down to earth (she didn't even wear a white coat). She wasn't preachy or patronizing, and she didn't try to make me feel shitty about my decision not to take tamoxifen. I really liked her (do like her), and it's a good thing, since she'll be feeling me up every year.

Chapter 12

My breast surgeon is on the lam

I GOT A LETTER from my women's health center (a group practice specializing in breast surgery and gynecologic oncology) that my breast surgeon, Dr. Cutter, had left the practice.

What? Wait. How? I don't ... Why? No!

Just when I'd gotten used to Dr. Cutter, I'd have to start over with a complete stranger who was going to fondle my boobs and not laugh at my jokes. That sucks. I've found that the more often I meet a person, the more comfortable I am taking off my shirt for them. Now I'd have to start all over again and introduce my breasts to someone new. Dammit.

Also, why did Dr. Cutter leave? Was it a mutual decision, or had she been *asked* to leave? Was it something innocent, like texting at work? Or was it professional negligence? Had all her patients' boobs exploded a year after she'd treated them? I performed a quick self-exam on my left tit. Was it growing? I was beginning to feel a little fevered and dizzy. I put the letter down, and my stomach went a bit funny. I felt like I might need a poo. I couldn't believe I was about to survive six months without advanced breast cancer, only to die from an exploding tit caused by a microbial infection that my surgeon (who had probably just fled the country) picked up in Burundi on her last mass-slaughtering holiday.

How many of her patients had already died? I got all *Murder She Wrote* and frantically typed search phrases into Google: "breast surgeon kills patient" ... "breast surgeon suspected of infecting patients' breasts with exploding microbes" ... I even tried "breast surgeon extradited to the Ivory Coast to face trial for serial killings," but I stumped Google.

I began to worry that maybe the fault didn't lie with Dr. Cutter at all. Maybe she left because she could no longer work for such a shoddy women's health practice. Maybe she'd watched too many of her fellow surgeons kill their patients, and she couldn't take it anymore. No, if that was the case, surely she'd have sent me a letter of warning? Er, wait, they probably made her sign a non-disclosure agreement. Crap, I bet she moved to some country in Europe where they have socialized medicine, and where there's no profit in performing unnecessary surgeries. Now I'm stuck with a bunch of greedy doctors who will want to biopsy my uterus next. (I seriously wrote that last sentence before I even knew what was coming the following year. I don't want to give away too much about what happened, so I'll just give you a hint. The name of the procedure starts with "hyster" and ends in "-ectomy." I must be fuckin' psychic. Or psycho. Like a broken watch that's right twice a day, I've worried about so many things, one of them is bound to come true, eventually. But this is a complaint for another book.)

Still, I couldn't help smugly telling Fran, "See, remember that fruit-flavored vodka cleanse and going-to-Mozambique-with-Doctors-Without-Borders-to-kill-patients thing I was telling you about? I was right. Look, my surgeon left the practice under a cloud of suspicion." I threw the letter at him.

He read the letter and said, "It doesn't say anything about a cloud of suspicion."

"I KNOW!!! IT'S A COVER-UP!"

Chapter 13

Wherein Karen worries about an upcoming MRI, public restrooms, and shitting herself—generally in that order

THIS WILL COME AS a big surprise to you, but I started worrying about my breast MRI weeeeeeeks in advance. I had gotten a prescription for Xanax in anticipation, but I'd taken Ativan (another drug for anxiety) for a previous MRI, years before, and it hadn't helped at all, so I wasn't particularly confident that Xanax would help me to overcome my claustrophobia.

During the last MRI on my neck, my head was locked in a fixture, so when they started rolling me into the tunnel on the conveyor, all I could think was, "What if this machine takes a shit?"

I wouldn't be able to get out, because my head would be stuck, and I certainly couldn't leave *that* behind. (Could I?) I wouldn't even be able to scooch out, because I couldn't raise my head high enough to remove it from the contraption—the tube had *literally* no head clearance. If we lost power, I was going to be *figuratively* fucked.[137] Fran couldn't even pull me out by my feet. I'd be trapped.

What made matters worse was that the MRI room was on the basement level, which meant that if the building was bombed by a terrorist, it would take weeks for them to dig me out.

Holy fucking get me out of here, Batman! I didn't want to be buried alive for weeks! (I would be the worst Chilean miner ever. What a nightmare!) Plus, it wasn't like I was part of a stranded rugby team and could start eating my compatriots while awaiting rescue, because I was pretty sure if the hospital got bombed, that fuckin' nurse was going AWOL.

The claustrophobia overtook me. I started to panic, but I was also feeling terribly embarrassed about having to press the panic button so soon. My first thought was that I should try to meditate and see if that would calm me down. Unfortunately, this was immediately followed by the thoughts, "Nope" and "Get me the fuck out of here."

I very heroically overcame my embarrassment and started pressing that God. Damned. Button like I was on the *Price Is Right* and knew exactly how much that toaster oven cost.

Press. The nurse didn't respond. Had the bombing started? *Press, press, press.* Still no word from the nurse. Good Lord, how

---

[137] N.b. *That's* how the words *literally* and *figuratively* are used, kids. But also, "n.b." is an abbreviation for nota bene, which is Latin for "note well," which I, embarrassingly, didn't learn until I was in my forties. I think it's how they said, "FYI" back in the olden days. It sounds less aggressive and snarky than "for your information," doncha think? This book should be required reading for high school English classes, (which is something else you should mention in that Amazon review you're working on, which is literally writing itself at this point).

bad was it out there? *Press press press press press press....* An interminable amount of time passed, in which I forgot to breathe and then died. I found myself in a tunnel with a distant, bright, warm light that I really wanted to go toward. Then I heard my dead grandmother greeting me: "Are you all right in there, Mrs. McCool?"

Only my grandma sounded just like the nurse asking me a really stupid question. Of course I wasn't all right. You don't press the shit out of the panic button if you're all right. Did she think I was ringing her to tell her how much I was enjoying the test so far? The voice came through a small, tinny speaker. Obviously that fucking nurse was far, far away and monitoring me from the safety of a bunker.

I answered, "Yes, fine, but ..."

I didn't mention how stupid her question was or ask why she left just as the building was being bombed, because she was probably in on it. Better not to let her know that I knew, or she'd have to kill me to keep me quiet. Looking back, I thought she had looked a bit terroristy, with her brown eyes[138] and her black shoe-bomb–hiding sneakers, but I said nothing. *(Dammit. If you see something, say something, Karen!)*

"I just need to get out. Now." I said this in a tremble-y and slightly squeaky way that would brook no further delay. Before I had a chance to yell, "I SAID NOW! YOU UNTRUSTWORTHY, BROWN-EYED, BLACK-SNEAKER–WEARING TAINT SNIFFER!" She said, "Okay."

It took thirty hours (or seconds) before the conveyor belt started rolling me back out. Fucking stupid slow nurses and their stupid slow conveyor belt things. They're the real terrorists.

---

[138] Is insinuating that brown-eyed people are terrorists kind of racist-adjacent? It's hard for me to tell since my eyes are blue, so I'm part of the master race.

I left, then I had to make an appointment at another location to get an "open MRI." Thankfully, the second facility was on the first floor of a one-story building, and the machine was more like a table than a tube. It was open on all sides, so I wouldn't be trapped, and none of the nurses looked exceedingly suspicious,[139] so *that* MRI went swimmingly. An open MRI is just like lying under a table, which I did a lot of as a kid. The biggest difference was that I hadn't brought any crayons, so I couldn't do any dog drawings on the ceiling of the machine. (Their loss.)

So, in remembering how awful the first, closed MRI on my neck turned out, I was determined to go directly to an open MRI for my breast. Awesome. I had a plan. I called to schedule it, but the secretary told me there was no such thing as an open MRI machine for breasts. (*Shit.*)

However, the nurse *assured* me that the newer machines have a much wider opening with more headroom (presumably, in case I had to make a hasty exit), and I wouldn't have to put my whole body in it, since they were taking images only of my breasts and not of my abdomen (halfway out already ... that's good). It didn't sound too awful ... until she told me I'd have to lay facedown in the machine. (*Motherf—.*)

So, while I could escape, I'd probably be sick. I should explain. I sometimes have dreadful bouts of vertigo. It can be triggered by something as simple as bending over and turning my head to one side to look in a cabinet. Once, I was lying facedown on a deck chair, reading a book, and when I got up, the whole world was spinning. And yes, I realize the world does, in fact, spin (smartass). But although I'm no Neil deGrasse Tyson, I do know you *aren't supposed*

---

[139] The nurses had brown eyes, but they wore white sneakers, like normal people.

to feel it. I narrowly avoided throwing up, but I was nauseated for a day and a half. So, even though I might not feel prohibitively claustrophobic, lying tits down in this MRI machine was still going to suck. Figures.

Of course, other than the obvious fear of physically getting through the MRI, I was also exceedingly worried they'd find something in my right boob, and I'd have to go back to square one with another core needle biopsy, like *Groundhog Day*[140] from hell, starring my right tit this time instead of the left. Honest to God, if they made me start this process all over again with a new cancer scare, I was going to have to commit hari-kari. (Errr ... actually, is it still considered hari-kari if you stab someone else?)

Unfortunately, medical procedures aren't the only thing I worry about. There are a multitude of things that scare me and make me feel stabby. As mentioned, having to shit in a public toilet is one of them. I don't even like *peeing* in public toilets, but I *really* dread having to shit in one. This is partly due to the necessity of using the "hover" technique, which is not a position conducive to a satisfying poo. Also, I'm always concerned about "the splashback." Can you get an STD from toilet water? I don't want to find out.

By the way, when I hover, I direct my tinkle *into* the bowl, ladies. Like a World War II bomber, I only release when a high-value target (the center of the bowl) is in my sights. There are far too many ladies out there who don't appear to have very good aim, or they act like they're dropping fuckin' napalm, with little care for mass casualties. (And it's always the elderly and the young who suffer when tinkle is left on toilet seats.) What's up with these women? They must be repulsed by piss on the seat or they wouldn't be hovering in

---

[140] If you haven't seen it, *Groundhog Day* was a movie starring Bill Murray in which he kept repeating the same day over and over.

the first place, so why would they leave their pee droplets on the seat for the next person to find? Uncouth much?

Oh, and here's another pet peeve of mine: basic shitaquette *demands* that you never leave a floater in the bowl. (Leave no soldier behind, 'cause *semper fidelis*?) And further, you should perform an extra courtesy flush if you left skid marks in it. Do I really have to tell anyone this?

Besides that, there's the sheer disgustingness of going into a public restroom where the previous occupant left a horrendous cloud of stank. Then, as I leave, I always feel the need to clarify with the next person I pass, who's on her way in, that "I *swear* it wasn't me."

But she probably doesn't believe me. It's like when your dog *really did* just fart. So now, the next person in line for the bathroom thinks I'm a stinky, rude blamer of other people for my own stank. Nobody wins. (Except the original stanker, who got away scot-free.)

You know what else creeps me out? Smelling someone else's farts. A friend once told me that a fart is actually tiny shit particles in the air. That there is a fine example of information I did not want to know. After learning this, I couldn't even breathe through my mouth if someone farted, because the only thing worse than getting shitty fart particles in your nose is getting shitty fart particles in your mouth. I have to hold my breath, and it's impossible to hold it long enough to pee, wipe, wash my hands, and escape the bathroom. I end up using the turtle-shirt technique as a make-shift gas mask, but the front of a shirt is not the best filter in the world. Plus, then my shirt has concentrated shit particles at the location where I inhaled, and it's gross to walk around for the rest of the day with someone else's inhaled fart residue right below your face.

If there are no other options, and I absolutely *must* shit in a public toilet, I try to find the one with the least amount of traffic. (I have *shitting shyness* and I can't squeeze one out if there's someone in the bathroom with me.) It needs to be a little used bathroom, so no one can possibly identify me by my sneakers when I leave. I don't know why I care so much what other people think, but I do. I guess it's something drilled into girls from a very young age, which is a terrible curse to put on a kid, really.

Thankfully, my own shit doesn't stink.

LOL. I'm joking! Of course my shit smells ... it smells like citrus.[141]

Then there are those annoying self-flushing toilets. The kind that go off randomly and prematurely if you don't hold perfectly still in your squatting position. It's as if the toilet is telling you, "Off you go then, luv. Fanks ever so much, but that's you done now, innit?"

They're always rushing you, and for some reason, in my head, they all have little old British lady accents. Some of them flush really violently and end up spraying you with a mist of pee-filled toilet water, too. I hate it.

I have the exact opposite problem with automated sinks. They *never* come on. No matter how many times I wave at them. They have a middle-aged British man accent and sound like I'm horribly inconveniencing them every time I want to wash my hands. They're like "Ye shure ye need a do all 'at? Quit bein' such a posh wanker and feck off. A can' be bothered. And if yer was usin' ta toilet paper proper, yer wouldn't need yer 'ands washed now, would ye?"

And those automatic hand dryers.... Bah, what a waste of wall space. I usually give up after about five seconds and wipe my hands

---

[141] 'Cause I use Poo~Pourri original. (Believe it or not Poo~Pourri is actually a thing. You spray it in the water before you shit and it traps the stink. I highly recommend it.)

on my jeans. In my head, automatic hand dryers sound like an American teenaged girl. They're like, "You want me to do whaaaat? Dry your haaaaands? Mmmm ... do I haaave to? Wut ... ever."

Then they roll their eyes, and only the tiniest bit of air comes wafting out.

How about we take a poll? Which is worse: those huge, heavy toilet paper rolls the size of Saturn's rings, or the metal contraptions that lock up two normal-sized rolls of toilet paper like they're the fuckin' Crown Jewels? The big, honking roll is a pain in the ass, because it's so large that it's impossible to get it rolling by pulling on the paper, which is thinner than Bruce Willis's hair. You only get a tiny square at a time because the roll won't rotate. The only option is to lean over and push the roll with one hand (very awkward while trying to maintain a hover—which come to think of it, may explain all those pee drops on seats), while you use your other hand to prevent any paper from hitting the floor, because then you'd have to throw away a ten-foot section and start all over. (If it touches the floor, the disgustingness travels up the paper a few feet. That's science.)

The double roll system works okay, but only for the first roll. The problem begins when the "spare" is called in for backup. You have to reach up into the metal box like a kid trying to get a free Snickers bar from a vending machine. It's almost as if the public toilet caretakers are *trying* to discourage wiping in public restrooms. Why do those people hate clean butts so much?

What exacerbates my public bathroom phobia—and this is uncomfortable for me to talk about, so please bear with—is that ever since I had my gallbladder removed, I occasionally have problems with—oh, let's just call it *urgency*—when I have to shit. Are any of you familiar? When it sneaks up on me, I need to be *really* close to a

bathroom. I'm not gonna lie ... getting caught in public in this particular predicament has made me mildly agoraphobic. If I go out, I
have to plan far in advance. Can't eat any spicy foods the day before
(ask me how I know), and I must have taken my daily shit before I
can leave the house, or I'm not going. I *really* don't want to shit in a
public bathroom (or any bathroom other than my own, if I'm being
honest). I know, I know. TMI. And it's terribly humiliating. If you
tell *anyone* about this, I'll probably shit myself.

Gawd.[142] Let's all just shut up about it, already.

Oh, but wait ... before we shut this down, I have a shitty story
to tell you (and I wish that was a euphemism). When Fran and I were
vacationing in Maine one year, I ate some bad clams (not on pur-
pose. I wasn't like, "Garçon, please bring a dozen of your finest New
England Tainted Clams." Though I might as well have). We were
staying in a little bed and breakfast on our way up to Acadia National
Park, even though I hate staying in B&Bs. They are waaaay too inti-
mate. I prefer an impersonal hotel where the lady who checks me in
isn't the same person who cleans my toilet.

So anyway, after dinner, Fran and I went back to our room, and
within an hour my stomach felt like I'd swallowed a hot coal straight
out of a BBQ grill from hell. Massive heartburn. Not long after, I
started to call Huey on the big white telephone. I continued yarking,
pretty much nonstop, for what must have been an hour. As I was on
my knees praying to the porcelain God of Abraham, Isaac, and
Yackup, hurling my offering into his throne, all of a sudden, I felt it.
(Uh oh.) I lifted my head and thought, "Hunh?"

The grenade pin had been pulled and my other end was about

---

[142] Fran said spelling "gawd" with an "aw" was okay once in the book ...
but it was getting old with repetition, which is strange coming from a guy
who can eat a turkey and cheese sandwich every day for lunch for thirty
years.

to detonate. I'd been betrayed by a fart in the past, and that's a mistake you only make once ... which I think is what Maya Angelou was referring to when she said, "When you know better, you do better."

As quickly as I could, I turned myself around, got my pants down, and barely made it in time to avoid a natural disaster in my pants (and a very awkward next day at a laundromat). It was a narrow escape. My ass, which by this time could have been used as a rocket launcher, successfully achieved touchdown (ass onto seat) with only a half a second to spare. I was high-fiving myself as I heard the agreeable sound of rushing shit hitting water. (Which is a whole lot better than the sound of rushing shit hitting pretty much anything else.) Sweet relief. The eagle had landed.

I felt like I was shitting out the entire cast of *Game of Thrones*.[143] All three states of matter (liquid, solid, gas) were escaping from my ass like a science experiment gone horribly wrong. I may have levitated. But the celebration of my pants-removing dexterity was short-lived. Although I was relieved that my exploding ass was safely ensconced over the turdlet, I soon realized I wasn't done vomiting and was too far from the sink to accomplish both tasks simultaneously. I hurriedly searched for a trashcan, and I found one, but ... it was fucking wicker! Who uses a wicker basket for a goddamned bathroom trashcan? Morons who run B&Bs, that's who.

The baby Cheesus must have been looking out for me that day, though, because at the bottom of the basket was a small, folded-up plastic bag. Thank the Good Lawd, and let the multitasking commence. (I'm not a religious person, but I did say a little prayer of thanks to baby Cheesus for the barf bag.) I spent the entire night

---

[143] If you haven't watched this TV series, the cast is ridiculously large. One beta reader (Robyn) wasn't sure if I meant that there are a lot of cast members or that the actors in the show are crazy big. I meant both. It was a lot of shit y'all.

shitting and vomiting. Woo hoo. Yay vacation.

We had to leave the B&B the next morning to drive further up the coast to our next destination, and I knew checking out was going to be awkward. I had been hurling quite loudly (according to Fran) and also, apparently, I had been belting out curse words between the phrases "oh dear God" and "sweet Jesus, not again" the entire night. I guess I didn't realize how loud I was, but I don't think, even if I had known, I'd have cared much. I thought I was dying.

The next day, I asked Fran, "Do you think anyone else staying here heard me?"

He said, "Karen, the entire town of Kennebunkport heard you."

I punished that bathroom. I may have made the wallpaper curl. I tried to clean it as best I could, but I didn't have any cleaning supplies or paper towels. I dumped what vomit I could out of the plastic bag into the toilet, and I tied the top of the bag closed, but after looking around again for some reasonable place to dispose of it, I regrettably had no choice but to place it back in the wicker basket.

Our entire room smelled like a Porta Potty. On the last day of a crowded carnival. In August. Where vendors served turkey legs with a side of gastroenteritis.

I left a very large tip on the dresser and made a hasty walk of shame straight to the car as Fran went to the front desk to get us checked out. It was a very crappy shituation. I'm not sure the HUGE tip on the dresser was any consolation to whoever ended up cleaning our bathroom since they probably still have some of my shit particles stuck in their nose to this day. (If it was *you*, I am soooo sorry!) I will never *ever* be able to show my face at that B&B again, and if I'm being honest, in most of New England.

For all these reasons and more, I fear and despise using public bathrooms (which include B&B bathrooms), and I'm also still pissed at that friend for relaying that awful shit-particle trivia. I don't know which of these things makes me the most anxious ... having an MRI, shitting in a public bathroom, or getting food poisoning while staying at a B&B. But if you held a gun to my head, I'd probably pick having the shits while stuck in an MRI machine. That would be horrifying. And I had many weeks to worry about it.

Chapter 14

Fuckin' insurance companies

THEN, THE MOST FRIGHTENING thing to date happened. Even more terrifying than having to shit in a public toilet and cancer scares combined (according to Fran). We got a "denial of coverage" letter from our insurance company.[144]

After my lumpectomy, I started receiving letters from our insurance company, saying they were denying coverage. We had signed up for a new plan months before, and our new policy began on January 1, which was the same month all these tests and procedures started. The letters basically said they were denying payment for pretty much everything, and the total amount I would be responsible for was over $25,000. Can you believe all this shit cost over twenty-five grand, and I didn't even get a new set of perky hooters out of the deal?

The "Remark Code" for all the denial-of-coverage letters was as follows:

---

[144] Fran says this is EXACTLY the type of situation that entitles one to freak out.

"The patient's coverage does not provide for this service when performed by an out-of-network provider. Therefore, no payment can be made for this service."

The back of Fran's head exploded. We had specifically chosen this insurance plan because our local doctors and hospital were in "tier 1," meaning they are preferred providers and would be covered with minimal deductibles. We confirmed this by looking on the insurance company's website (Fran checked a hundred thousand times, 'cause he was freaking out about the bills). But still, according to their letter, our hospital was out of network.

Fran called the insurance company, got an automated recording and was immediately put on hold (or placed in the fifth circle of hell). After about fifteen minutes, he got another recording: "Due to inclement weather, our offices are now closed."

Okay, fair enough. We'd just had a major snow fall the night before.

So, I called the next day and was, surprisingly, put on hold. It was one of those typical "on-hold recordings" playing on a loop: "We are now experiencing extended wait times. We apologize for this inconvenience. You can also go to our member portal at www ..." which essentially translates to this:

"Hello, caller. You don't stand a chance of getting through to us any time soon. That's right. Wait if you want, but it's gonna be awhile. Hope you didn't have any plans for this afternoon! You may or may not get to speak to a human, eventually. We're still deciding, but based on that curse word we heard you utter as this message began (we can hear you), we're leaning toward not. It would be best for everyone involved if you'd hang up the phone, dig around on our website for a while, and see if you can find an answer you like there, 'kay? Thanks. Here's some shitty music we hope you don't enjoy."

While I was on hold, I decided to document the entire phone call for my book.

WARNING: I fear some parts of this passage are going to be highly offensive. I don't mean them to be, but still, they probably are. So maybe you should stop reading right now. But if highly offensive things don't bother you, read on. Not that I'm absolving myself of any offensive shit in advance. If you *do* read this and you *are* offended, it's still my fault (even though I tried to warn you). I hope you aren't offended, though ... fer realz.

So here I am, working on my book while on hold, and to my insurance company I say, "HA! You thought you were going to waste my entire afternoon, discouraging me from ever calling you again. But I'm a multitasker. Look at me getting something else done! Who's the loser NOW, insurance company?!"

(Still me. I'm the loser. Listening to the worst on-hold-muzak, evah).

* * *

I just spoke to a very nice woman named Makisha in 'premium support' (I bet she's not an annoying WASP). After I gave her my insurance member number, she quickly apologized and said my account was being handled by a different department, and she'd have to transfer me.

My mistake! I must have accidentally pressed the number for 'premium support,' when my plan clearly only allows for 'shitty support.'

I expect she'll transfer me to "Joe" next (a.k.a., Vijaykumar): "Let us try turning powver off and den back on."

(That was me typing with an Indian accent. Is that racist? This whole book is turning into a hate crime.)

* * *

Oh! Fabulous, *another* pre-recorded update: "We are experiencing extended wait times ..." etc, etc. So annoying. When they say "we," I *know* they really mean "me." *They* aren't doing any waiting at all. The entire customer service department is probably having cake and cookies in the break room.

* * *

I've now been on the phone for forty-five minutes.

* * *

Sigh I wonder what kind of cookies they're eating. I bet they're homemade.

* * *

I'm bored.

* * *

I can't believe they didn't offer me a cookie.

* * *

You know what would be fun? If they put all the people who are on hold on a "party line." We could each share what medical procedures we had, then bond when a really good song comes on. "**Oh ... migod**, I love this song!" (see "old ass")

"Shut up! I love this song, too!"

"This song is my jam!"

But then the song "My Heart Will Go On" from the movie *The Titanic* would start playing, and some asshole would begin singing along to it, and then I'd wish I was back on hold again.

* * *

Oooo ... wait. Now I'm talking to Gary. He keeps putting me on hold, but he's nice. He sounds like Samuel L. Jackson in *Pulp Fiction,* only a lot less anger-swear-y. And much, much younger. Crap ... is that ageist? Or worse—racist? I hope it's not racist. I wonder if I should ask Gary?

* * *

After looking at the website's list of tier 1 hospitals and reviewing my plan, Gary thinks he'll need to re-submit the claim. He asked if he could put me on hold again. I wanted to say, "By all means, move at a glacial pace. You know how that thrills me," but I didn't want him to think I sounded like Meryl Streep's snooty character in *The Devil Wears Prada*. Only older.

* * *

Gary's back. He said he reprocessed the claim. I just needed to allow seven to ten business days for it to go through. (I bet what he really meant was that I'd need to call again in a couple of weeks to start the whole thing over again, because it was easier for him to delete the entire claim than to do anything about it.)

In insurance-speak, "reprocess" means, "Keep bitching and maybe we'll pay you. Eventually."

Well ... I was only on the phone for an hour and ten minutes! That wasn't terribly painful.

I'd rather you stick a fork in my eye.

(Just kidding. Please don't stick a fork in my eye.)

A few weeks later, I got a letter denying payment for the anesthesiologist. I should have called the hospital and demanded that they reduce this charge, since their promised "twilight sleep" was more like a "fitful unrest." Instead, I made another hour-long call to my insurance company.

The insurance company eventually paid all of my claims, but it took three months and at least six phone calls (I lost track) like the one I described above, as well as wading through multiple claim denials, with various reasons for rejection, all of which made me want to fight club my own face.

Many folks who fear universal health care often cite government inefficiency as the main reason, as though large private companies are paragons of efficiency. They don't want "big government" getting between them and their doctor. I guess they think rich CEOs, with a profit motive, make better middlemen.

I tried to look up the salary of my insurance company's CEO (because I was on hold with those fuckers once again, and I didn't have anything better to do). The most recent data I could find was from 2008, when he was earning close to three-million dollars a year—and that was just the CEO. The COO made close to two million, and another five of the top executives made close to five million, combined. That's a lot of denied lumpectomy claims. Most people would consider themselves lucky to retire on just one year of a CEO's salary. People who think companies are efficient should perhaps try calling a private health insurance company to figure out why they're being denied claims for coverage they've already purchased. At the very least, it will give them some time to catch up on emailing friends, or to write a memoir, which is a great way to spend a few afternoons.

It certainly gave me time to further reflect on what makes me anxious vs. what makes Fran anxious. Me: Medical procedures. Fran:

Paying out of pocket for medical procedures when you already have insurance. Oy.

Chapter 15

The breast MRI—there will be bruising

AROUND SIX MONTHS AFTER my lumpectomy, I was finally scheduled to have my first breast MRI. For the entire drive there, I kept hearing the song "Bravely Bold Sir Robin," from *Monty Python and the Holy Grail,* playing in a loop in my head.[145] I'd taken a Xanax an hour before I left (mostly because my appointment was at 2:15, and 1:00 would have been a little too early to start drinking on a weekday). It wouldn't be an exaggeration to say I had been dreading this since I first learned I'd need to have this test. Among other things, I was afraid of embarrassing myself with my claustrophobia and wasting everyone's time.

When I got to the radiology office, the lady at the front desk said she didn't have my paperwork. Amber alert! No ... RED ALERT! What the fuck? Should I call 911!? My oncologist's office

---

[145] Here's a link to a YouTube video of the song, but if you haven't seen this movie, you seriously need to go get some culture: https://www.youtube.com/watch?v=jYFefppqEtE

202 | Karen McCool

told me weeks ago that they'd send the order for the MRI directly to radiology. I was freaking out because I didn't want to have to come back another day. I had already spent a good month worrying about this visit, gerddammit, and I wanted to get it over with.

I called the oncology office. (They *never* answer their phone, by the way, which is tragic, because when you're dying from cancer, who has the time to wait for a call back?) I left a message on their answering machine and waited, nervously, assuming they wouldn't get back to me in time and I'd have to reschedule. But on that particular afternoon, Lady Luck was with me. An oncology nurse called me back within a few minutes and said she had just faxed over the script.

Well color me flabbergasted. I was glad the crisis had been averted, but I sure could have done without the added stress. My life expectancy dropped by about ten years on that day. My hair didn't turn completely white afterward, but I definitely started looking more like a cast member of *Golden Girls* than of *Friends*, is all I'm sayin'.

Then Lady Luck took the rest of the day off. I was led back to some changing rooms and handed a gown (*not* a salmon one). I was then asked to sit in an exam chair to be prepped.

A nurse named Dave told me I would need a contrast agent halfway through the MRI, so he needed to give me an IV. He then proceeded to do an *atrocious* job of giving me an IV. I was ready for the initial prick of the needle, sure, but I hadn't expected Dave to miss my vein entirely. Undeterred, he pushed the needle in deeper. Still no luck. He then switched his angle of attack from forty-five to eighty degrees. Nothing. With the needle still in my arm, he tried angling it in different directions. (Can veins hide?) *Fuckin' ouch, Dave!* Not being one to walk away from a fight, Dave continued this angling and poking like he was searching for lost Spanish gold.

I'm no expert, but I didn't think Dave was going to hit any veins where he was poking. He was shoving the needle into the middle, inside part of my forearm—nowhere near the usual point of entry inside the elbow. *Dafuq, man? Cheesus, were you an oil driller in a previous life or what, Dave?*

It reminded me of that movie *There Will Be Blood*, where Daniel Day-Lewis played the ruthless owner of an oil drilling company. Dave was merciless. *Dude, that may be how you find oil in Texas, but you're not going to strike blood by jabbing a needle into any ol' spot on my arm.*

After his epic failure on my left arm, where the bruising was beginning to obscure the search area, Dave went to plan B, and decided to drill into my other arm. *Fuck me, how long are we going to play Find the Vein before you go after my jugular, Dave? Do you sleep hanging upside down?* (This is when I started calling him Vampire Dave in my head.)

I know what you're thinking, and you're right, I *am* a big baby, but it fuckin' hurt! (Shut up Fran. It did, too.)

For his next attempt, Dave poked the needle into my inner elbow area. You know, that bendy place where there's *always* a vein? *(Yeah ... ummm, 'scuse me for asking, Vampire Dave, but shouldn't that have been plan A?)* Finally, things began to progress relatively smoothly. A vein had been tapped, and access to my bloodstream was achieved. Good thing, too, because I wasn't going to wait around for him to try fracking next. #CheckPlease I'd have stomped back to the front desk in my hospital gown to demand a refund. And it's really hard to stomp in paper booties.

Oh, and is this weird? Vampire Dave's pointer finger was sticking out of his purple latex glove! It's not just me. That's totally weird, right?

Granted, I didn't look at his finger too closely. I had my head turned away the entire time he was aggressively stabbing me with the needle, so I suppose it's possible that he had a flesh-colored finger condom on it, but I don't think so. Why would he do that? The whole (and hole) thing freaked me out, and I rather wanted to assault him with a pillow.

After this thorough (and unsanitary?) arm stabbing, I went back to the MRI room to begin the next torture. The MRI machine resembled the escape pod at the beginning of the first *Star Wars* film (the *real* first *Star Wars* movie. The one with all the cheesy special effects that I still love). As advertised, the MRI tunnel, where I'd need to lie facedown, was fairly high and wide, and it was open on both ends. The diameter of the tunnel was much larger than the older machine, where I had panicked years before, so I felt a little reassured. (And I do mean *"a little."* Like on a scale of one to "get me the fuck out of here," I was at a seven.)

Before I got into the machine, one of the radiology nurses asked me to show her the site of my lumpectomy so she could mark the location with a sticker. I still had an angry red scar, so I just opened my gown and said, "See if you can guess." She found it.

Technically, I have two scars on my boob, if you include the one from the original core needle biopsy. The scars give my boob character. My tit looks like a shady badass who gets into a lot of knife fights. In the made-for-TV miniseries, my boob should be played by Michael K. Little, the guy who was cast as Omar in *The Wire*.

The radiology nurse handed me two earplugs. I told her I thought they might make me feel more claustrophobic, but she said I had to wear them. Shit! She then had me lie facedown on a conveyor belt, where there was a raised, uncomfortable plastic ramp for my torso. The ramp had two boob openings. My tits hung down through these holes like a couple of upside down whack-a-mole heads. The conveyor belt then slowly moved me into the tunnel.

When I felt my arms touch the sides of the tunnel, I said, "Just because I'm paranoid, if this machine loses power, will you be able to get me out?"

The nurse said, "Absolutely. There's an emergency release."

I didn't ask what would happen if the emergency release didn't work, because this line of questioning could last all day, and I just wanted to get this the fuck over with already.

I kept my eyes closed, but I wasn't completely paralyzed with claustrophobia, because I figured this kind and compassionate nurse would surely help me out if there was an emergency. Like, if a mass-murdering gunman entered the building, the nurse would help me get to safety. Then I thought, *tomorrow, after the tragedy, we'll have a reunion, and we'll hug each other and cry about all the other people who were lost in the disaster, and we'll vow to do something meaningful with our lives*, except then I remembered I wouldn't have time to do anything meaningful, because I was probably dying of breast cancer. Fuck. (We now return you to our regularly scheduled panic attack, already in progress.)

The MRI machine was *not* built for comfort. Let's just say the Spanish Inquisition would have resulted in a lot more converts if they'd used MRI machines (or core needle biopsies, come to think of it) along with "the thumbscrew" and "the rack." The plastic ramp had started digging into my ribs and sternum after about ten minutes. The worst part, though, was the circular pad/toilet seat for my head. The nurse offered to add more padding to it, but that would have made it worse for me. I can't tilt my head that far back, because of my herniated disc. So my neck was in a bad position for the entire procedure.

By the way, this particular MRI machine, in addition to making lots of knocking noises, also emitted an occasional alarm-type shriek. It sounded as though someone was playing with a *Star Trek* soundboard app and kept pressing the fucking "red alert" button. I opened my eyes, briefly, but all I could see was the plastic bottom of the MRI tunnel, which was a few inches away from my face. *Yikes! Close your eyes, Karen! Close your eyes! It only* feels *like you are trapped in the trunk of a shuttlepod!*

Then I thought maybe that red-alert sound was a "Cancer Tumor Alarm." *When the nurses come rushing in to take me to the on-site emergency cancer surgery operating area, I am definitely going to shit myself.*

I eventually stopped my mind from wandering down this mental rabbit hole by singing John Denver songs in my head.[146] Don't judge me. "Rocky Mountain High" is calming. Also, John and I used to be engaged.[147]

After the MRI was over, I stood up and felt a little dizzy. My vertigo had kicked in, but it wasn't terrible—just enough to make me feel a bit queasy. My neck and shoulders were sore, and I looked silly as fuck when I left, because I had deep red marks on my forehead from the conveyor belt's head-cushion-that-was-anything-but-cushiony. (Later that evening, the really bad shoulder pain started. Naturally. Aggravated discs are aggravating. I fucking *knew* that machine was going to cause me problems afterward. Oy.)

But what was really odd was what happened on my drive home. The nurse told me to stay hydrated after the procedure to help flush out the contrast dye they'd injected, so I went to a McDonald's drive-through and ordered a small lemonade. After I drank about half of it, I started shaking like an LA office building during a magnitude

---

[146] I hope I only sang them in my head, although, if not, it would explain why I thought I heard the nurse say, "Bye, Calypso," as I was leaving.

[147] In my head. When I was twelve. He was going to leave his wife Annie for me.

9,073 (or greater) earthquake. Only worse. I felt reaaaally cold, and the shakes started to get so violent that I had to pull into a parking lot.

I remembered a nurse had asked me before the MRI if I had ever had a reaction to the contrast agent they used, but I had no idea, since my last MRI was for my neck, and I didn't recall getting an injection. So, great, was this some kind of bizarre allergic reaction? I was *freezing*, even though it was the summer and the temperature was around 81 degrees outside (even hotter in my car). I called Fran, because I wasn't sure I should drive, but he doesn't answer his phone when his wife is probably dying from a freakish reaction to an MRI contrast agent. (I bet if I was calling him to see if he needed anything from the supermarket, he'd have picked up.) I waited it out in the parking lot and, after about ten minutes, the shaking slowed down enough for me to drive home.

I laid down on the couch, covered myself with a heavy blanket, and was still shivering an hour later. My teeth were chattering like one of those wind-up teeth-chomping toys. I looked up the contrast agent online. Shaking wasn't listed as a side effect, so who the fuck knows what *that* was all about? Very odd. For half a second I thought it might have been because I wasn't used to taking Xanax and, when it wore off, my body freaked out. But that had never happened before, and I'd taken Xanax on numerous occasions. It was peculiar and anxiety provoking. And what the hell? As if it wasn't bad enough that breast cancer was trying to kill me, the MRI contrast agent was taking a whack at scaring me to death, too.

As I mentioned, my neck had flared up. I know it's bad when the pain extends into my shoulder. That means my herniated disc is impinging on the nerve that goes down my arm. I called my GP's office the next day to see if she could give me a refill on my Percocet prescription. The nurse told me I had to make an appointment for a visit, because the doctor needed to see me to refill my prescription.

Mind you ... it's a herniated disc ... inside my neck. There is nothing for the doctor to "look at" or "probe" while I'm in the office. I usually sit there for five minutes and answer questions that I've already answered a million times before, while the nurse practitioner types on her laptop. Obviously this gives her time to catch up on her Twitter, because what could she possibly be typing that I haven't already said? My answers remain the same, then she finally writes me a prescription.

And okay, I get it—they want to be sure I'm not abusing pain meds, but the last time they had prescribed Percocet for me was six months earlier, and they'd given me fifteen pills. I'm not a pharmacist, but I don't think fifteen fucking pills are enough to keep anyone high for six months. Do you *really* think I'm abusing the drug? Do I look like a drug addict to you? Well, maybe you should stop judging people by the way they dress then, asshole.

I asked the nurse if I really *had* to come in. Nothing had changed, there wasn't anything new for the doctor to see unless she wanted me to do *another* MRI on my neck to see if the discs had magically repaired themselves, which would be pretty fuckin' amazing, since I needed pain meds *because of* the last MRI. I told her I'd just paid a $250 co-pay for my breast MRI the day before, which is why my neck was now hurting, and I'd have another $100 co-pay next week, when I went to my oncologist for a follow-up visit, and do I *really* need to come to the office to see my doctor, for an additional $40 co-pay, so she can write me a refill on my prescription? (Resulting in raising the cost of my pain pills from around $25 to $65, because my insurance didn't cover prescriptions.) So yeah, I was angry and in pain and I didn't want to have to get dressed and drive myself to the doctor's office. The cold fish's response was, "Yes."

Infuriating. At this point, I was thinking my next book should be a murder mystery. Or, more accurately, a true crime novel, because I was feeling a bit homicidal maniac-ish.

The only good thing about visiting my GP to get pain meds refilled is that there's no physical examination involved, so I didn't have to shave my legs. #SilverLinings

Oh, I almost forgot to tell you ... later, when I went to the pharmacy to get my refill, there was a young-ish (late teens/early twenties), gay man behind the pharmacy counter. Don't question how I knew ... I knew. And my gaydar is impeccable. Honed to perfection way back in middle school while in the choir. Mama knows a fabulous gay man when she sees one. So, as I handed the twink my prescription, he asks, "Do you have any health issues?"

Health issues? Now I'm thinking, "Oh grrrrl ... you haven't looked around? You're working in a pharmacy."

But instead, I said, "I have a herniated disc *and* I'm probably dying of breast cancer. How long do you think the wait for this prescription will be? I've got a shit ton of Oprah's *Super Soul Sunday* shows on my DVR to get caught up on, and I may not have much time."

He blinked at me in response.

I paid for the pills, then left the store to start my entire week of worrying about MRI results. My MRI had been at 2:15 the day before, and I should have scheduled my follow-up oncology appointment for 3:00 the same day. I hate waiting. I went back to singing "Bravely Bold Sir Robin" on my drive home.

Chapter 16

The MRI results and another visit to the chocolate factory

S O BACK I WENT to the chocolate factory (the oncology office) to get the results of my breast MRI and to find out exactly when I would die, fer realz this time. There were a few people in the waiting room who appeared to be very sick, and I found it deeply unsettling.[148] How long before that was me?

I had been talking to Steve about my fears, and she told me not to start worrying *hard* until they told me I had stage IV cancer (when it starts spreading throughout your body), because Steve is wise. I started a new mantra. It went like this, "Breathe in, hold, exhale, and relax. You're not in stage IV. Breathe in, hold, exhale, and relax. You're not in stage IV. Breathe in, hold, exhale, and please don't let me be in stage IV. Please Lord Cheesus don't let them tell me I'm in stage IV, and relax."

---

[148] I wonder if oncologists get sick and tired of all the sick and tired people they have to see?

This only helped a little. The scary oncology office was still scary.

By the way, Steve gets me. She never offered platitudes like, "Don't worry. I'm sure you'll be fine."

Some folks, trying to be helpful, would tell me about someone they knew who had breast cancer, who is fine now. Gah! You might think that would be comforting to hear, but for me, it wasn't. It felt more like they were pooh-poohing my fears. I knew that not everyone who ever had breast cancer was fine. Many women die of the disease. Countless others suffer from long-term health consequences as a result of their breast cancer treatment. Steve understood that the process was scary, and she never tried to minimize what I was going through.

I continued to have a nagging feeling that the proverbial shit was making a beeline for the nearest fan. I'd certainly been much luckier than a lot of other DES daughters, many of whom had to deal with vaginal cancer when they were children/teens or with a cervical cancer diagnosis in their twenties. The precancerous cells on my cervix and in my breast were caught early. Still, in many ways, I felt even less prepared to deal with any kind of medical issue than I was in the beginning. I now knew how shitty all these surgical procedures really were. I guess you never know which medical scare will completely undo you, and I was still feeling very undone.

The prospect of more surgery and a potential cancer diagnosis still frightened the shit out of me. (That was not a euphemism. My stomach was upset.) I felt certain this MRI or my next mammogram would show some shadow (if you squinted at it just right) in my right boob, and I'd have to go through this all over again. Truly terrifying. I suppose I could chalk it up to just feeling vulnerable, since my left boob had only just begun to feel completely healed (I had been getting infrequent, stabbing pains in my breast, which is apparently normal), but I didn't think I'd ever be able to stop worrying about breast cancer.

The night before I got the results, I talked to Fran about how I was just going to *die* if they saw something on my right boob and I had to start over with another core needle biopsy, then lumpectomy. While I'm on the topic of dying (and I know—when am I not, right?), I've told Fran that I want to die before he does. There is no way I could deal with his death, so I asked him to promise not to die before me, but he refused. (So inconsiderate.) He had some bullshit excuse about how women live longer than men, and he's already five years older than I am, and blah, blah, blah, but we both know it's because he's not as committed to this relationship as I am.

Fran texted me just as I sat down in the oncology waiting room (see screenshot below):

While sitting in the waiting room, the song in my head was, "Look Out (Here Comes Tomorrow)," by The Monkees.[149] It got

---

[149] Honestly, I've mentioned so many songs, this book could easily be made into a musical. Someone call Lin-Manuel Miranda. (He's the guy who created and starred in the Broadway play *Hamilton*. If you're old and if you haven't seen this musical, it might be because all the music is hip hop and someone thought you might have a fucking heart attack if you ever saw George Washington being played by a black man.)

stuck in my head the day before. For a brief moment, the song "Seasons in the Sun," by Terry Jacks, almost supplanted it, but I quickly nipped that in the bud. *'Cause I am a fucking optimist.*

I was brought back to an exam room to wait for Dr. Tumorstein. I looked at the massive bruise on my arm where the nurse, only a week before, tried to rape my vein with his needle. And yeah, I don't like rape "jokes" either, but that bastard truly assaulted my arm. It was eight days later, and I still had a massive, dark purple bruise (see picture below. I added the state of Texas next to it so you can see that my bruise was roughly the size of the Gulf of Mexico).

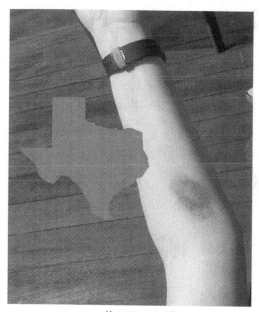

Drill, baby, drill!
(My arm looks like the goddamned BP oil spill.)

Fuckin' Vampire Dave.

Finally, Dr. Tumorstein came into the room and said, "How are you, Mrs. McCool?"

"Depends on my lab results."

"Oh, they didn't tell you? Everything looks fine."

Wait ... what the fuck? Who are these people who could have saved me *days* of torment but never called to tell me everything looked fine? Can you introduce them to me, and also, can I borrow your clipboard? I'd like to smack them each on the forehead with it. Fuck.

So, thankfully, it was good news. Dr. Tumorstein didn't see anything that looked suspiciously breast cancer-ish, so I wouldn't need another biopsy. Thank Dog,[150] and also, *Fuck yeah!* I had finally passed a test! I learned something else about myself that day: Some people hold their anxiety in their stomach or shoulders ... I hold mine in my ass. I could feel my butt unclenching just the tiniest bit after hearing the good news. I was a half-inch shorter when sitting down.

After seven months of stressing out and fearing the worst, it seemed I could finally take a breath. I properly exhaled for the first time in forever. I didn't even realize I'd been shallow breathing. Finally, my breast cancer scare had come to ... well, not a close, exactly, but a deferment.

Would I ever be able to truly relax again? I was the tiniest bit hopeful. After all, my cervical cancer scare had been twenty years ago, and I hadn't had an abnormal Pap smear since. Things were looking up, and so, with encouraging MRI results in hand, this shitty journey appeared to have resulted in a pretty positive outcome (or a temporary stay of execution, if you're cynical like me).

---

[150] Robyn said I might want to mention that Dog and the baby Cheesus are my religious idols so people don't think I'm insane. Thanks Robyn. I'm sure that'll do the trick.

This book started with me making end-of-life plans, and now we've arrived at the surprise ending, where I never actually had cancer. (Surely you didn't see this coming what with all the unexpected plot twists and turns?) I do hope you like happy endings, 'cause if not, you just got hosed....

Or did you?

If this book were a horror movie, this is the part where the credits start rolling and the camera slowly pans over an empty front lawn ... the lawn where we *should* see a very dead bad guy, because we saw him fall out of a second-story window. The camera then turns to our heroine, and we watch her through the first-floor window, where she is celebrating her survival after the "death" of the bad guy. But we, the audience, know he's still alive. Whereabouts unknown. And y'all know what that means.

There's gonna be a sequel. Yup. The following year brought more problems. Cancer-scare problems. Involving *all* my lady-parts. (Insert sad-trumpet sound effect: bwaa bwaaaaa.)

Goddammit, Cancer, why won't you piss off and die!

END SCENE

Epilogue

The end?

I'VE BEEN TRYING TO decide what I want my last words to be. Steve Jobs' final words were "Oh, wow." Somewhat profound, but I found myself wanting more. Did he mean, "Oh, wow, this afterlife is fucking amazing"? Or was it more like, "Oh, wow, oblivion sucks"? I need details.

As my parting gift to Fran, when I die, if I can still talk, I'm going to describe everything I see. If I encounter a warm light at the end of a tunnel and my dead grandparents, I'll be sure to let him know. If I get a glimpse into Narnia, I'll even do a quick sketch if he hands me a Sharpie and a piece of paper. Though, if there's a hell, there's a distinct possibility my last words will be "Oh, shit."

Hopefully, I'll have something weighty and eloquent to say, but if my final words are simply, "I love you," I could do worse.

As for coming up with some parting thoughts for this book, I'm finding myself at a loss for words. Well, okay, I'm not at a total loss ... in fact, to those of you wondering why a woman *who didn't even have breast cancer* wrote a book *mostly about breast cancer*, my farewell words would be, "Fuck off. I thought I had breast cancer."

Besides, isn't it about time *someone* wrote a memoir about *not* having breast cancer?

Breast cancer is some scary shit, yo. Even if you find out you don't have it after you were sure you did, it's still terrifying. For a neurotic mess, the phrase, "You have an increased risk of getting breast cancer" sounds exactly like, "You're gonna die from breast cancer someday real soon." Not having it yet is only marginally less scary than having it now, because I probably do have it now and just don't know it yet.

See? Equally alarming.

But if you or a loved one has been diagnosed with breast cancer, my final words here would be, "I know a friend of a friend whose mother had breast cancer and she's totally fine, so don't worry and just think positive thoughts!"

J/K! (I made myself cringe there.)

What I mean to say is I am so terribly sorry you have to deal with this incredibly frightening disease and all the horribly upsetting procedures and treatments that are involved in trying to survive it. I can't even begin to imagine what you're going through. If you are one of those people who likes to learn as much as you can about breast cancer and your treatment options, my friend Steve highly recommends reading *The Breast Book*, by Dr. Susan Love. I suppose it'd be a good start.

I hope science finds a cure soon. In the meantime, I hope you come through it with a minimal amount of anxiety,[151] a maximal amount of humor, and a good support group around you. And for sure, you should start with being your own support group of one. Be kind to yourself. Maybe even find an internet community of women who are dealing with breast cancer. You are not alone.

I wish you a complete and speedy recovery followed by a long, happy, healthy, and joy-filled life. May you live to be a ripe old lady (well, not ripe ... you should maybe keep bathing).

---

[151] Ha! Said the president of The Worry Club for Women (member since 1980). Remember, I'm not only The Worry Club president; I'm also a client.

If you're in hospice, I wish you peace, hope, love, and the ability to squeeze out a little laughter in every moment you have on this earth before embarking on your next journey. And also, you should probably call my friend Steve. She's amazing.

So here's the part in my story where I reveal all the things I learned from (not) having cancer. But I have to come clean ... I didn't learn much, other than that I'm an incredibly squeamish crybaby. I certainly didn't learn anything you don't already know. I can only offer a few thoughts about life that are already so evident that if they were clues and you were Nancy Drew, playing the game *Clue*, you'd say, "Duh, it was clearly Professor Plumb, in the library with the candlestick." In other words, things that are so plainly true you'd scream, "Thanks, Captain Obvious!" if I gave voice to them. But, whatever. At the risk of repeating what you already know, or of sounding trite or schmaltzy, here are a few things I've learned over my time here on this tiny, fragile planet, and that I wish/hope for you.

NOTE 1: This is not me offering advice to anyone who had or currently has cancer. That would be an invitation to punch me in the face, and well you should! These are just my own personal hopes for you. And for everyone, really. So, if I talk about finding peace, and you really hate peace, fuck it, raise some hell! I can get behind that. I don't want to tell you how to live your life. Rock on whicher bad self!

NOTE 2: I learned all these things from other people.

(Other people can be sooo smart!)

Here's the list:

Peace

I wish you peace. Find it, cultivate it, and choose it. (I know, right? This one can be hard.) When that bastard in his big, honkin' SUV cuts you off, you can either get super pissed, or you can choose peace. Try choosing peace. (I also flip him the bird, but that's just me.)

~ *I learned this from Thich Nhat Hanh's book, Peace Is Every Step.*

Live fully

I hope you live fully. Be present and be well, but also ... sometimes ... put down the kale and eat your favorite foods, even if they're full of sugar, or fried, or aren't gluten free. Drink lots of [insert favorite alcoholic beverage here] and party like there's no tomorrow (except don't forget there probably will be a tomorrow, and if you have a lot of shit to do, you may not want a hangover, so ... you know ... maybe plan ahead a little). All good things in moderation, sure, but sometimes ... fuckin' tie one on and get silly. Enjoy life. It's too short to spend doing shit you hate. What I'm trying to say is make good choices, kids ... but sometimes, don't.

~ *I learned this from my dogs, who live fully every day.*

Don't be a dick

I hope you will be kind to others (and, just as important, to yourself). The most profound thing my dad ever taught me was the golden rule, and he said it like this: "Do unto others as you would have others do unto you." In short, don't be a dick. And I know, right? I definitely need to work a little harder on this one. Here's something that might help: I had a teacher in college who was from India and was a Hindu. In class, she once shared her belief that everyone we meet has helped us in some way in a previous life, so meeting them again in this life is our chance to repay that kindness. (That's why she became a teacher.) Imagine if we all treated everyone we meet as someone to whom we owe a debt of kindness. Crazy awesome, right?

~ *Learned this from my dad and from a college professor. Totally worth the price of tuition.*

Love

I hope you love in as many ways as you can. Love yourself, love another person, love a pet, love writing, love drawing, love winning pie-eating contests, love being alone, love being with other people, love crop-dusting[152] when you're at the mall ... okay, maybe not that last one. (No one wants your shit particles in their nose.) My point is that it doesn't matter who or what you love, just that you love with as much joy and passion as you can muster. Then rinse and repeat. I once had a friend at work who always complained about men. She said, "I just want a man who adores me." I didn't say it at the time, but I thought, if you want to be adored, be adoring. If you want to be loved, be loving. I learned this from my husband. He excels at this.

~ *Learned this from Fran.*

Let it go

I hope you are able to just let it all go. Especially shit from the past. Don't beat yourself up. You aren't your past actions or mistakes. My mom used to play John Denver on our shitty old record player when we were kids.[153] #GuiltyPleasure In one of his songs, called "Sweet Surrender," he sings, "There's nothin'

---

[152] Crop-dusting is when you fart while walking. Sorry!

[153] Hey kids, "record players" were old-timey contraptions used to play music. Back when you couldn't shuffle-play your songs and had to listen to an entire album *by one artist* from start to finish, like God intended.

behind me and nothin' that ties me to something that might have been true yesterday." That's good to remember, too, I think. It's a new day; you can make new choices. Believe that. Also, for me, surrender means letting go of wanting to control shit I have no control over. (I need to remind myself of this *constantly*.) My grandmother used to quote an old Scottish saying: "Whit's fur ye'll no go past ye!" (Whatever's meant to happen to you will happen). I give myself permission to worry. I'm allowed to be scared, as long as I remember to also ... finally ... let it go. In college, a professor once told my class, very fervently, "Just let it go!"[154] It struck a chord with me then and still does. It feels true to me—maybe to you, too.

~ *Learned this from John Denver, from my grandmother, and from a teacher.*

Laugh

I hope you laugh and I hope you do it often. Seek it out. I learned about laughter from watching Saturday morning cartoons as a kid, and I continue to learn the joys of a good guffaw from many hilarious women like Miranda Hart, Mamrie Hart, Melissa McCarthy, Kristen Wiig, Wanda Sykes, Nikki Glaser, Jenny Lawson, Tina Fey, Betty White, Kathleen Madigan, Lily Tomlin, Amy Poehler, Lola, Beth, Steve, Amy Schumer, and oh, shit, now I've started a list and will forget to name someone, so let's end this now by simply saying, these ladies, and so many others like them, can make me pee my pants from laughing, and then make me laugh harder because I just peed my pants. Ain't no shame in it. Pursue the kind of laughter that when you try to tell someone else "what was so funny," you laugh so hard

---

[154] And to my beta reader Robyn, no I will not apologize for this section making you sing the "Let It Go" song from *Frozen*, you weirdo.

you cry and start talking in a voice so high, you can't be understood, and then Fran's like, "What?" That kind of laughter. Find it *like it's your job*.

Laughter truly is the best medicine. Especially if you can laugh at yourself.

It never hurts to laugh. (Unless it hurts when you laugh, then don't laugh.)

~Learned by doing.

XO,

Karen

Addendum

A word of caution

I FIGURE THIS BOOK needs to include a warning to potential readers about some of my foul language and offensive content. I feel obliged to insert a severe warning, so I'm doing that here. Forewarned is forearmed! Then why is it at the back of the book, you ask? Well, I wouldn't want to scare anyone off from buying it, now would I? Duh! If you bought this book without checking for warnings first, well, we both know whose fault *that* is.[155]

This book is not for the squeamish. This is going to be a harrowing tale containing graphic descriptions of boob mutilations. Also, if curse words make you cover your mouth in horror, you should read no further. This book may contain strong language, and by "may," I mean "does," and by "strong language," I mean I am in an abusive relationship with the word fuck. (I'm the abuser.) The only words I like better than "fuck" are "fucking" and "fuckity." I like them best when they are all used in the same sentence like, "Fucking fuckity fuck this sentence is marvelous." The only sentence I can think of that I might like better would be, "Here you go, Karen: These mint-chocolate brownies prevent cancer *and* make you lose weight." But seriously, I curse a lot. It's like I have that rare symptom

---

[155] It's mine. Totally my fault. I'm sorry I tricked you into buying this book. But also, no take-backsies.

of Tourette's, called coprolalia, where the sufferer engages in uncontrollable cursing ... only I don't try to control it, because I like dropping f-bombs. (Here's one in the drawing below.)

You may wish to seek cover.
There's about to be a profanity 'splosion.

Also, if you are a woman who was recently told that you need a breast biopsy, and you're a little anxious about it, you probably shouldn't read this. It would be like watching the movie *Jaws* before going for a swim in the ocean, or watching *Psycho* before getting in a motel shower. It's pretty much guaranteed that you won't read what you were hoping to read in this book. Unless you are hoping to read that you should never, ever get a breast biopsy because they are incredibly abhorrent, and you want some (any) justification for not having the biopsy done. If that's the case, read on, my friend. (But you should probably get that biopsy anyway. Just sayin'.)

Parts of the book will be incredibly offensive to many—including, but not limited to, doctors; Irish people; Jewish people; WASPs; my husband; my dogs; grammar Nazis; any person whose joke I may have inadvertently pilfered, then butchered (sorry, Lola); anyone named Kaitlyn, Brittany, or Ashley; anyone who named their daughter Kaitlyn, Brittany or Ashley; everyone on Fox News; people who watch Fox News; Tea Partiers (okay, those last two were redundant[156]); most of my friends and relatives; and all other humans. The book will also contain some violence and nudity. Well, probably not any *actual* nudity ... but I did write one paragraph on my cell phone while taking a dump. Maybe "partial nudity" would be a more accurate description, since I had my pants *on*; they were just around my ankles. I apologize (after the fact) for putting that image in your head. I'm really very sorry.[157]

One more word of caution: There may also be some fairly juvenile fart jokes and pooping anecdotes, and I think I should be honest with you. If you don't enjoy a good fart joke, first of all, that's the saddest thing I've ever heard, but secondly, it's probably not going to work out between us.

I'm advising viewer discretion, but in consideration of those readers who have delicate constitutions, I will mark all the offensive parts by using the Adobe Garamond Pro font, so you can skip over

---

[156] That was for those who enjoy redundancy, repetition, restatements, or redundancy. You're welcome.

[157] I'm not really "very" sorry. I'm only the slightest bit regretful. You can hardly blame me for your mind coming up with gross images. I'm as creeped out as you are.

them if you'd like. Again, if you see Adobe Garamond Pro type, like this, you will know you should skip ahead.[158] No need to thank me. I'm a giver.

(Fran, please remember to add "She was a giver" to my obituary. Also, are you allowed to have footnotes in an addendum, or am I a groundbreaker, too? "A giver and a groundbreaker..." Write that down, Fran.)

---

[158] Yes, the entire book is printed in Adobe Garamond Pro. That's the point, you delicate fucking flower.

Glossary

Also called the "assistance for old people" section, or "old ass"

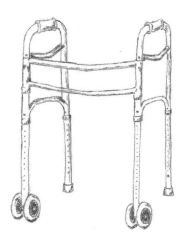

THIS IS THE PART of the book where an attempt is made to define slang words or to explain pop culture references, but quite frankly, it's just as likely that this glossary will only add to the confusion. Ah, well, fuck it. This entire book has been one long exercise in godawful explanations. Why not add a few more pages to lend some final disorder to the mess? Once more unto the breach, dear friends.

A glossary example

Well done, you. You've mastered the art of clicking on a hyperlink. Again, if you're reading an electronic version of this book, you can click on the glossary term (in this case the above hyperlinked phrase, "A glossary example") to return to where you left off in the text. Alternatively, you could continue reading the book from this point forward, which would certainly free-up your afternoon, and if we're being honest, you won't have missed much.

Click regret

This happens when you click on a link on the internet and regret it the second you're taken to the new page. Like, say you were searching for pictures of Canadian beavers to use as a reference for needlepointing a beaver onto a pillow, along with the words, "I don't give a dam." You find a link that looks promising, but when you click on it, you're taken to a porn site. (Regrettably, this is how you learn that the word "beaver" isn't used exclusively to describe semiaquatic rodents.) The first feeling you have may be shock or bewilderment, immediately followed by click regret (or possibly delight; I'm not here to judge). Click regret can also happen when you hastily click on a Facebook thumbs-up button, because you thought the poster was saying something disparaging about Donald Trump, but then you realize they're actually agreeing that Mexican immigrants are rapists and murderers. You immediately "unlike" the post, but you're worried the poster already got a notification that you liked it, when you didn't. You hated it. And "unliking" something is not *nearly* as satisfactory as giving it a thumbs-down, so you're mad the rest of the day because Facebook and Twitter are ruining our lives with their lack of thumbs-down buttons. Thank gawd YouTube gets it or we'd never find relief.

Cray

This is short for "crazy." The kids dropped the letter "z" to turn this two-syllable word into one syllable, because it's all about economy of language when texting, I guess? You would use this in a sentence like, "Mabel puts shredded coconut in her chocolate chip cookies, 'cause that bitch be cray."

Dafuq

This is short for "what the fuck." It's usually said in the form of a question, with a slightly flabbergasted tone, as in, "Hearing aids cost how much? Dafuq?"

Death Star, hyperspace, lightsaber (and other Star Wars references).

A Death Star is a large spaceship, about the size and shape of a small moon, from the Star Wars movie universe.

Hyperspace is a mode of travel that gets you someplace faster than the speed of light. It's even quicker than that new bypass you're always complaining about, and it didn't require any exasperating road-construction delays. I'm not sure exactly how hyperspace works, because I'm not a sci-fi nerd who makes up fictional methods of travel, but from what I gather, you don't need to yield to enter hyperspace, which practically eliminates the main cause of road rage. Also, I believe I ended up cutting out the paragraph that used the word hyperspace in this book, but I enjoyed writing this definition so much, I decided to keep it.

A lightsaber is like what you'd get if a samurai sword had a baby with a carbon dioxide laser. My apologies for having used these and maybe other Star Wars references throughout the book, but if you haven't seen any of these movies by now, it's because those who know you have already concluded you would hate them. Otherwise, they'd have encouraged you to watch them a long time ago. I agree with those people. Don't watch any Star

Wars movies now. Just reconcile yourself to the fact that all references to Death Stars, lightsabers, hyperspace, etc., will hold absolutely no meaning for you. Besides, while this is almost as bad as not knowing what a Hobbit is, it would totally suck if you started watching the movies with *Star Wars Episode I: The Phantom Menace*, as you'd presume you should. But you shouldn't. If you did, the whole Leia-kissing-her-brother-Luke scene would really creep you out. (Unless, of course, you're in one of those weird families that always kiss on the lips, and if so, ew. You guys are gross.)

Duck lips

When someone, usually a woman in her teens or a Kardashian, is taking a **selfie** (see "old ass") with a camera phone, while making a kissing face, she is said to have "duck lips." As you may have guessed, this is because puckered lips look very much like a duck's bill. Some women think it's hot. It's not.

Emo

This is short for emotional. It's mostly used to describe first-world teenagers who have everything, but are super melodramatically depressed because their parents are so lame and life sucks because nobody understands them. You can identify emo teens by their nonconforming, black dyed hair (which they *all* have) covering one eye. Also, they typically wear black eyeliner. On the boys it's called guy-liner.

FFS

This is an abbreviation of "for fuck's sake." It's an uncouth alternative to "For God's sake" or a fairly excellent alternative to using the Lord's name in vain, depending on your perspective.

FML

This stands for "fuck my life." Generally, over-privileged people use this phrase to complain about really important things, like when they ordered a grande half-caff frappucino with vanilla and got mocha, instead, and wouldn't you just want to die?

Hashtag

The # symbol is called a hashtag. In this context, we aren't using it as a pound or number sign, nor as a "sharp," if you're a musician. It's used on social media sites as a sort of category designator or conversation tag, so everyone writing or tweeting about a specific topic—for example, the "suckiness of getting old" would use the hashtag, #gettingOldSucks, so any person who wants to discuss its suckiness can read what others have tweeted about it. Another example is if you want to share something you find amusing with the internet, you might add the hashtag #hilarious to your comment or post. Anyone can create and use a hashtag. Using hashtags is fun and has also become a way to make a brief comment about your own comment. For example, when describing this glossary definition, I might end it with #horribleExplanation.

And my apologies, but I couldn't think of a way to define hashtags without talking about social media applications, tweets, and the internet. I don't think people ever used hashtags on telegrams, did they?

Hipster

This is usually a white person, born between 1980 and 2000-ish, who typically lives in an urban environment. Hipsters eschew modern fashion and instead wear thrift-store clothes and skinny jeans. They often rail against corporate America while sipping Starbucks coffee without intending to be ironic.

Internet friend

Internet friends are people you meet through social media, like Twitter, Facebook, or online forums, but whom you've never met in real life. The best thing about internet friends is that you never have to invite them over for dinner. I highly recommend trading in your real-life friends for internet friends. You won't have to come up with another poor excuse to avoid uncomfortable social invitations for the rest of your life.

IKR? or ikr?

This is short for "I know, right?" For example, if someone were to type: "These adult diapers are a lot less bulky than I thought they were going to be," you'd type back in response, "IKR?" It signifies agreement.

imho

This is short for "in my humble opinion," and ikr? WTF? People who use imho are very rarely humble. (My own modesty requires me to meekly submit that this is purely my own estimation of the offender's apparent lack of humility. I may be wrong, and they might be exceedingly humble, as I am. But am I wrong? I doubt it.)

Interwebz

This is a colloquial term for the internet. If you don't know what the internet is, I'm afraid there's nothing I can do to help.

J/K or j/k

This stands for "just kidding." Let me try using it in a sentence: "Having a glossary for older people was a fabulous idea. J/K. This idea totally sucked. I might as well try to teach you how to record a TV show."

Justin Bieber

Justin Bieber is a popular young singer, and also a bit of an ass, imho. No, really, I am being humble and it's just my opinion. And by "my" I mean everyone who is not a teenaged girl. His fans are known as "Beliebers," because many are like freakishly obsessed cult members. And don't anyone tell the interwebz that I said Justin Bieber is a bit of an ass, because the Beliebers will destroy me.

kthxbai

This is short for "Okay, thanks. Bye." It's generally used as more of a dismissal than as an actual expression of gratitude, as in "Not everyone likes Justin Bieber or his music. Let's all calm down about it, kthxbai."

LOL

This is an abbreviation for "laugh out loud." When someone types LOL, you can be fairly certain they are only mildly amused. At the most, they may have chuckled a little, but they never *actually* laughed out loud. LOL is over-used (similar to OMG), and people need to stop it. It was originally used in text messaging, but it has become so ubiquitous that you will now hear people vocalize it, as in "Ell, Oh, Ell," which is extraordinarily irritating.

I realize I just used the phrase "text messaging" in this definition, which may have caused you to scratch your head. In an attempt to keep this brief, I'll define text messaging as a form of written communication, usually transmitted by cell phone. And I know that sounds ridiculous, because we're holding a phone and could easily call and speak to the other person, but we prefer sending brief strings of horribly misspelled words and abbreviations that can be easily misinterpreted, because that way, we don't have to speak to anyone. Text messaging is a form of socially acceptable antisocial behavior for those of us who hate talking to people. And welcome to the future. The English language is now dead.

Moar

This is a cross between "more" and "roar." Here's an example of its most common use: "I need *moar* cookies."

No biggie

This is short for "No big deal." If you grew up in the fifties, it has replaced "no sweat." If you grew up in the thirties, you're probably thinking, "What's your story, morning glory?" but it's just another way of saying, "It's not a problem." The section of the book that used this phrase was edited out, but I kept the definition in the glossary because it amuses me.

Noodge

I think this is a Yiddish word, meaning an annoying person, or someone who pesters or nags. For example, "I don't want to use a cane. Stop being a noodge."

Oh ... migod

This is another way of saying "Oh my God." There is a significant pause after the "oh," which then turns these three words into two. It's used to convey a strong sense of shock or disbelief, as in, "Oh ... migod, did you hear Myrtle got an STD within a month of moving into that assisted living place?" See also "OMG."

OMG or OMFG

These are abbreviations for "Oh my God" and "Oh my fucking God." OMG is used in excess, mostly by teenaged girls to convey a sense of shock or disbelief. As in, "OMG, did you hear the new Taylor Swift song? I just died." See also "Oh ... migod."

One Direction

This is a boy band. You probably heard the collective scream of anguish when one of the band's five singers, Zayn Malik, quit the band around March of 2015. It was the fangirl scream heard 'round the world.

Poke

On Facebook, you can "poke" someone with a virtual finger. It's a way to let someone know you are thinking about them, but you're too fuckin' lazy to send them an email or text message. It's a great way to annoy a person from afar.

pwn

It essentially means "own" … as in I will "own you" or "you just got owned." It had been used to let someone know they were about to suffer a humiliating defeat in a computer game, but since the "p" key is right next to the "o" key on a computer keyboard, it has been mistyped so often that the new spelling, "pwn," was adopted. Here's an example of using the word pwn in a sentence: "I'm going to pwn that old bitch Tilly at the next Bingo game."

Selfie

A photograph one takes of oneself (sometimes with other people in it, but the person taking the selfie is always the primary focus). It's the main reason why putting cameras on cell phones was a bad idea. And also why our society is doomed.

Shade

"Shade" is typically used with the word "throwing" (i.e., "throwin' shade"). If you say someone is throwing shade, it means they are insulting or judging someone else. For example, Maude was always throwin' shade at Archie Bunker.

TED Talk

TED Talks are video recordings of very smart and interesting people, discussing their area of expertise. These talks are collected on the TED website. The videos are usually short, powerful, and inspiring, and they cover a range of topics, including science, education, creativity, writing, health, and global issues. The TED website says their mission is all about "spreading ideas." It seems they haven't yet gotten around to inviting pointless boobs to give talks, but I'm sure, when they do, I'll be the first one they call.

The c-word

Unfortunately, this phrase is often used as a way to avoid saying an indelicate, uncouth word that starts with the letter *c*, much the way people use the phrase, "the n-word." In this case, "the c-word" refers to a woman's vajayjay. The actual word for "the c-word" is too indelicate and uncouth for me to put in print, so you'll just have to make your best guess, because I'm too much of a fucking lady to spell it out for you.

Thug life

There are various definitions of this phrase, but I'm using it here to refer to someone who has led the life of a thug. Someone who had a difficult childhood, grew up in a ghetto, and who does whatever they need to survive. Someone who demands respect, doesn't take any shit from anybody, and knows you have to *take what you want*, 'cause as a young white girl growing up with two brothers in suburbia, I know all about thuganomics.

TIA

This is an abbreviation for "thanks in advance." It's used to sarcastically imply that the reader will immediately fulfill a request. For example, say you wrote a letter to your son who *never* calls you. You would say something like, "Don't forget to call your poor mother who went through seventy-two hours of labor when she had you. TIA."

TMI

This is an abbreviation for "too much information." If you feel like you want to start talking to your kids about your trouble passing urine, for example, don't. Because TMI. It's often used as a polite way of saying, "Oh, shut up."

Urban Dictionary

An online dictionary of all things slang (www.urbandiction-ary.com). Many of the entries are extraordinarily gross and not to be used in polite company. It's not for the easily offended, not for children under eighteen, and probably not intended for adults over seventy with delicate constitutions. Just sayin'.

WebMD

This is a website with medical and health information. It's where hypochondriacs go to find out what they're dying from this time.

WTF

This is an abbreviation for "what the fuck." Usually posed as a question. As in, "Did you see that awful color Mildred chose to dye her hair? WTF?"

Yelp

A website where any person can write reviews about restaurants, hotels, local businesses, etc. As a side note, YouTube has some hilarious videos of actors reading dramatized versions of Yelp reviews. Go to YouTube and search for "real actors read Yelp," and prepare yourself for a cracking good time. Warning: If you're anything like me, and I suspect you secretly are, you'll waste hours watching these "real actors read" videos—especially the unintentionally hysterical interpretations from Christian Forums. (Search for "RAR Christian Forums.") I, personally, would like to see more "RAR Facebook Status Update" videos as well. Hey, internet, you need to get on that.

Acknowledgements

THIS BOOK WOULD NOT have been possible without the help and encouragement (ranging from tepid to strong) from the following people, listed here so you'll know who to blame. (Now follows a bunch of thanks to people you don't know and inside jokes you aren't privy to, so no one would blame you if you decided to skip ahead to the "About the Author" page. Not that the author page is all that exciting, either. It might be just as well if you put the book down here and call it a day.) Oh, actually, there is a thank you below for anyone who read this book. I would love it if you'd check it out, but I don't want to be all bossy about it, so *you* decide. (It's called "Thanks for reading and halp!")

My first thank you is to Beth Evangelista, for being a huge pain in my ass until I agreed to write a goddamned book. I hope you're happy, Beth. But seriously, without your inspiration, and noodging, I never would have started this project and, now that it's done, I hope you'll join me in doing a victory dance (arms akimbo, of course).

Many thanks to Steve for all her patience and understanding when I'd bitch about how anxious I was, and for always talking me off the ledge. I'm forever grateful to have you as a friend.

To my beta reader Robyn Swift, thanks for letting me use the black George Washington joke and also for making me laugh daily on Twitter. I shank you very much for being the kind of friend who would help me hide a body, and I hope we can get together next Shanksgiving. Oh and hey, quick shout-out to my Twitter peeps #BloggessGang (you know who you are). I love you glorious weirdos!

So many thanks go to my friend and editor (who resigned from her position as an international spy under allegations of not doing any actual spying), Lola, for having to answer a million stupid questions like, "Which simile do you like the best?" and "Which is funnier?" and my classic, "Should I just delete all of this?" For the past two years, you've helped me turn this steaming pile of shit into the mediocre, mildly humorous book that it is today. Sorry for the disappointment. I know this writing project is "not soup yet," but sometimes, you just have to shoot the editor and go to print. For a long time, I didn't think this book would amount to anything, and I was right, but not for your lack of trying, Lola. I'm so glad our paths crossed on the interwebz. (For the record, all remaining errors in this book are entirely my own. I'm sure Lola told me to fix them, and I ignored her.)

I need to thank my mom and dad for their constant encouragement, and for showing me what it is to be a decent, kind, and generous human being. My sincerest apologies for my "teen years" (well, okay, teen through forties, if you insist). You are the very best of role models, and the world would be a better, kinder place if it had more people like Jerry and Margie Pucci in it. Thank you for being there for me, always. I love you.

Thanks go to my in-laws, first for raising such an incredible man, and second, for welcoming me so warmly into your family from the very beginning. As our hostess in the Outer Banks would say, "Bless your hearts." I love you guys.

I want to thank my niece and nephew for teaching me that love at first sight really is a thing. I loved you both from the first moment I held you, and it's fuckin' ridiculous how much I still love you two.

And finally ... thank you, Fran, my love. You're the only person I'd want to be stranded on a deserted island with. (And seriously, when are we gonna buy a deserted island?) I'm so thankful you married me 27 years ago, and I'm sorry you got hosed. (Sucker.) I love you more than Maggie loves squirrels and more than Fergus loves punishing other dogs. I'm the luckiest woman on the planet. Truly.

Thanks for reading and halp!

And for a final finally, I'd like to thank anyone who has read this book and **_halp!_** If you enjoyed this book or even if you didn't, please consider leaving a review on Amazon which is incredibly helpful for an independent author and can really make a difference. Since I decided not to submit to a large publishing house, I have no PR help, and word of mouth is critical. Please leave an honest review. Even if you hated it, it helps other potential readers to know what they may be getting into *before* they buy this book, which is a good way to avoid any misunderstandings (by those goddamned goody two-shoes who are horrified by a little cursing. Also, if they're looking for an *Eat, Pray, Love* level of delicious prose, they probably need to move along, 'cause there's nothing to see here).

Lord knows, my writing isn't for everyone, but I hope you enjoyed it and that you'll recommend it to others who share your impressive and refined sense of humor. Please rate the book and write a review on Amazon, however brief. (As a side note: If you know me in person, ethically speaking, you should mention that fact in your review, so readers know you may be biased when they see your very low rating.)

Also, can we talk? I'd love it if you'd swing by my website and say hey. There you can enjoy a lot more f-bombs and pointless dispatches from an anxious boob:

http://www.chroniclesofaboob.com.

Sign up to subscribe and get notified of new content on the website or when my next book is available. (And no, I will not give your email address to *anyone*. I hate all those spammy fuckers as much as you do):

http://chroniclesofaboob.com/subscribe_here/

Dive right in on the website and join in the conversation by adding a comment or two. Warning: It is BYOB. I personally think the website pairs well with raspberry vodka, but to each his own.

You can also find me on Twitter: @PointlessBoob.

Grab a drink, pull up a laptop, and let's get to know each other.

About the Author

KAREN McCOOL won the Nobel Prize in literature, never. She also never won a PEN/Faulkner Award or a Pulitzer, but one time she did win a PA lottery scratch ticket for three-hundred bucks.

All of the drawings and images in this book were created by the author. Some of Karen's other talents include being a concert pianist, having a photographic memory, teaching yoga, and lying about having other talents.

Karen is a former distance swimmer and was the first person ever to swim from Cuba to Florida without using a shark cage. Oh wait, that was Diana Nyad.

Karen lives in a yurt near Philadelphia, PA, with her husband, Fran, and their two dogs. Fergus and Maggie are both AKC Champions (the AKC stands for "Always Keepin [it] Cute"). Karen also enjoys making up a bunch of shit whenever she is asked to write a bio, then she just writes it in the third person, because she thinks it sounds more believable that way. She would be wrong. Thankfully, she doesn't do this for the entire book. She says you're welcome. Also, she's terribly sorry for the overdone joke about her author page being written in the third person. #SorryNotSorry

Made in the USA
San Bernardino, CA
07 February 2019